The Ocean World of Jacques Cousteau

Volume 14

The Adventure of Life

THE DANBURY PRESS

The earth awakens. The waters that formed the primeval seas and rainclouds came from deep inside the earth and emerged through geysers and volcanic vents. Modern geysers recreate the event every time they erupt in clouds of water vapor.

The Danbury Press
A Division of Grolier Enterprises Inc.

Publisher: Robert B. Clarke

Production Supervision: William Frampton

Published by The World Publishing Company

Published simultaneously in Canada
by Nelson, Foster & Scott Ltd.

ISBN 0-529-05159-1
Library of Congress catalog card number: 73-18796

Printed in the United States of America

23456789987654

Project Director: Steven Schepp

Managing Editor: Richard C. Murphy

Assistant Managing Editor: Christine Names
Senior Editors: Charlotte Willard
                David Schwimmer
                Robert Schreiber
Editorial Assistant: Joanne Cozzi

Art Director and Designer: Gail Ash

Assistant to the Art Director: Martina Franz
Illustrations Editor: Howard Koslow

Vice President, Production: Paul Constantini

Creative Consultant: Milton Charles

Typography: Nu-Type Service, Inc.

Table of Contents

The first living cell was little more than organized seawater. It reproduced and evolved about three billion years ago, thus giving a start to the great adventure of life on earth. Science predicts that favorable conditions will prevail for another four or five billion years: today is the YOUTH OF LIFE.

Life is an adventure, and its history is recorded in THE ARCHIVES (Chapter I), essentially the sedimentary rocks and the fossils they contain. The scientists who specialize in the study of these rocks and fossils are the archivists of life.

The modern concepts of evolution went through a long and painful development. When we look at the EVOLUTION OF EVOLUTION (Chapter II), we see the age-old struggle between science and theology, observation and faith, a struggle that in part parallels the course of evolution itself. Knowledge as well as species must evolve.

It's a tough world, as we're often told, and it is governed by an overriding principle: SURVIVAL OF THE FITTEST (Chapter III). Just as we adjust to various means to make our livings, the living creatures of the sea adapt to their surroundings. We depend on armies and police forces for protection, and in nature there are teeth and spines and some very unusual means by which the best equipped survive.

An evolutionary modification first appears as an altered gene in one individual. Only by passing on that new trait to one's offspring can a species change. Consequently EVOLUTION AND REPRODUCTION (Chapter IV) are immutably intertwined.

Evolution is not a unidirectional process that exclusively proceeds from simple to more complex forms. Along the way there are many divergences or EXPERIMENTS IN EVOLUTION (Chapter V) which lead to a fascinating array of offshoots from the evolutionary line. Such variants are essential and in the face of a catastrophe may yet take over as a basic stock for a new line of development.

The imprints and remains of life long dead provide us with clues to life in the past and its evolutionary procession to what we see today. Very limited in number but of profound interest are the LIVING FOSSILS (Chapter VI), which are living relics of past ages. These "missing links" afford proof that the guesses made about evolution are in fact founded in substance.

Introduction: Youth of Life

The development of the theory of evolution began with the question, "Where did I come from?" It is understandable that early man believed that he had been "created." How could he have guessed the age of the earth and understood fossils as the history of life recorded in stone. Many still do believe that the earth and life on it have remained essentially unchanged from the beginning. Change is new to man's consciousness. It is, even now, difficult to comprehend time on the scale of millions of years and almost impossible to grasp the few billions of years during which life has developed and progressed.

Erosion of the concept of a static world actually began as far back as the early Greek philosophers who felt that life-forms did change and give rise to new forms. But no proof existed until scientists began a systematic study of the layers of rock and the animal remains within. The collapse of old ideas came when Darwin, a religious man, became converted to evolutionism by evidence he saw in living plants and animals. The newly accepted concept of change both of land and life provided evidence from which we could search out our past and proceed with the detective story of man's origin.

Having realized that we share ancestors with monkeys and apes and that through our vertebrate relatives we are distantly related to starfish, we were able to delve further into ourselves. The birth of human consciousness is a good example. Evolutionary theory states that alterations in a species are solely the result of blind chance—random mutations that are most often lethal. We are told by psychologists that we use only a small fraction of the total potential of our brain. Is it possible that the evolutionary process had selected the most intelligent man-apes to survive but that random chance produced a mind with capabilities that far exceeded the needs of the animal at the time? Could our mind really be a preadaptation—a quality possessed by an animal not essential now but of vital importance to a future state of development? Or could it be another lethal mutation whose effects will doom the species at a future date? Philosophers are constantly torn between these two views. In periods of depression they see our mistreatment of other men, animals, and our planet, and become convinced that the faculty we call intelligence and conscious thought is a curse destined to bring about our downfall as a species. Personally, I feel certain our struggle to achieve, progress, and search the unknown is leading us to actualize hidden dimensions of our potential and will insure a positive future for mankind.

Regressive evolution is seldom a success; the system perpetuates those who move ahead. This is an important consideration when discussing our present-day evolution. Man has stopped his own evolution! The environment imposes few restrictions on us today; instead of selecting the most fit to survive, we select the environment to suit our needs. Our medical sciences heal the sick, allowing them to reproduce and pass inborn deficiencies to their offspring. Because of our higher states of consciousness, we consider ourselves humane and cannot supplement the forces of evolution by selecting the best of our species. In fact, our intellect may have rendered us incapable of even judging what is good or beneficial for our species. But it is our understanding of the basic principles of evolution and that same medical science which will permit us to play sorcerer's apprentice and cure the ills of mankind. Through genetic manipulation we can and will revitalize ourselves physically and, if our intelligence is a positive attribute, we will learn to use our mind and increase its capabilities to make life pleasant and worthwhile for everyone. Progress has already been made—an artificial gene has been synthesized.

In defense of evolution, I do not believe that its doctrine negates the existence of a divine being. It merely states that life arose gradually as a result of physical and chemical interactions in a primordial sea. In fact we have, even yet, no complete definition of "life." Recent experiments have taken inorganic chemicals and with the addition of energy as heat, ultraviolet light, or electric sparks converted them into amino acids—the building blocks of proteins. Other studies have found a "nonliving" broth of chemicals to aggregate, form spheres, grow and divide, giving an appearance not unlike some living organisms. It was recently proved that organic substances, such as hydrocarbons, are being routinely produced in outer space throughout our galaxy. These substances are turned into more complicated molecules that are the building blocks of proteins and of DNA in a catalytic process occurring during the formation of a star. The hypothesis of universal insemination of the cosmos is very promising. The question of "life" even arises when considering human beings. When the heart stops beating in a heart attack victim or when a yogi suppresses all brain waves, some may call them clinically dead but after revival both do live. Whatever life force was in them remained at least for that short period of apparent death.

The story of evolution is probably the most fascinating of all we have to tell because it reaches into our very fiber. It ties all forms of life together and provides us with a common bond to plants and animals. Basically we are composed of the same substances and possess the same basic drives, making us all brother in a cosmic experiment. Astronomers tell us that the earth should continue to exist for another five billion years. Since life has only been around for three billion years, we are still in our youth. The insights gained through the study of evolution will assure us a future and allow us to determine our destiny.

Jacques-Yves Cousteau

Chapter I. The Archives

The adventure of life as explored by man is truly a mystery tale. As in any good detective story, the evidence has been present all along but not until many apparently unrelated facts were put together could logical conclusions solve the mystery.

The story begins with "archives"—clues recorded in stone and available from man's beginning. Early Greeks questioned the significance of those animal imprints in rocks, imprints we call fossils. Large bones were interpreted as remnants of a former race of giants. More perplexing were the fossils of shells collected miles from the sea. Was it possible that these prints had "grown" in the

---

"As early as 450 B.C., Empedocles thought 'survival of the fittest' governed evolution."

---

rocks from seeds or that marine animals had crawled from the sea into the cracks in rocks? As Christianity became a prominent religious force, men found an answer to the question of how such marine animals got to mountain tops. They were carried there by the Great Flood. The biblical deluge would surely have caused the sea level to rise high enough for the creatures to invade regions presently far from sea. But a problem existed. It was Leonardo da Vinci who noted that clams whose remains had been found in Lombardy, 250 miles from the Adriatic Sea, could not have traveled the distance in the 40 days and 40 nights described in Genesis. His objections were discounted, and the assumption that those marine creatures found in rocks on land were proof of the Flood remained common until the 1800s.

The concept of change, in terms of a sequential development of life from simple to complex and of alterations in the earth's crust, has only recently been widely accepted. In the past there have been perceptive men of science who questioned the static, constancy of earth and life, described in the Bible as creation: "God saw everything that he had made, and, behold, it was very good." Any development of a new species or alteration in a land form would contradict this and doom the proponent of such an idea as a heretic. But as early as 550 B.C. some Greek philosophers thought that present animals and plants were the end products of many changes which had taken place over long periods of time and that life had become more complex during the process. Empedocles (450 B.C.) theorized that the fittest of nature's chance variants survived and the less fit were eliminated. Aristotle concluded that from generation to generation there was a tendency for a species to become improved. These early ideas on evolution preceded Darwin by 2000 years but were neglected and contributed little to the theories on evolution that exist today.

In the seventeenth century Nicholas Steno pulled together information about fossils and geology, showing the significance of strata and sedimentation. He felt, as did da Vinci, that fossils were remnants of past life-forms, which had become recorded in rocks very slowly. Steno realized that as particles carried by the sea settle, they become layered on the bottom, developing the characteristic strata of sedimentary rocks.

Opening the files. A stream erodes the sedimentary rocks, exposing them for investigation. For centuries man has marveled at the remains and imprints of life recorded in stone.

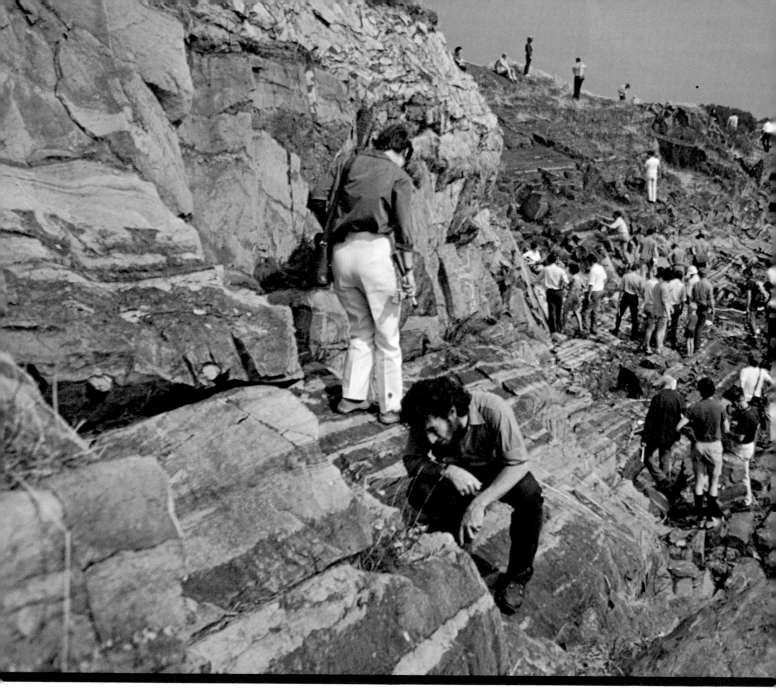

Written in Stone

Sir Walter Scott wrote about men who "...rin up hill and down dale, knapping the chunky stones to pieces w' hammers like sae many road runners gone daft. They sae it is to see how the warld was made." These people were geologists. Some specialized in the study of fossils encased in the rocks they were "knapping" away at, and these scientists were called paleontologists. All earth scientists are concerned with the history of the earth, but paleontologists particularly are readers of the story of life as it is found in the treasure trove of fossils.

The paleontologist heads out to the field, trusty hammer and notebook in hand, usually exploring backwoods and remote areas where all the bare rock has not yet been covered over with concrete. The fossil-specialist should be adept at mountain climbing, caving (spelunking), mapping, photography, drawing, surveying, and especially the arts of preparing and restoring fossils. These last

ample, a certain bone may be unknown in a certain fish, but a muscle on a nearby bone has left its mark to show where it must attach. The function of this muscle can be deduced, and the shape of the missing bone can be inferred. Many of the vertebrate skeletons in our museums are up to 90 percent plaster, but they are almost certainly accurate reconstructions.

When rock layers are undisturbed, young sedimentary rocks overlie older ones, and because of this the paleontologist can tell the relative age of his fossils by their position. Evolution is written in stone. The paleontologist possesses indisputable proof of past life with every fossil that he takes from the rock. The changing shapes of life can be traced through the rock records, across oceans and continents, through time and distance. A paleontologist holds the thread of evolution in his hands by combining the biological and geological evidence in fossils.

A scientific horde. *The sedimentary rocks (left) around the Oslofjord, Norway, contain a rich set of early Paleozoic fossils nearly 500 million years old. The study of a single subject by many specialists brings controversy, discussion, and answers.*

Alone. *It is usually impractical to have a whole party of paleontologists study remote areas, and the individual (below) must venture alone.*

two skills are vital, because the fossil that comes out of the rock often does not remotely resemble its true form until the mudstone or limestone casing (called the matrix) has been painstakingly removed. The usual tools for this are a dentist's drill and an engraver fitted with a fine point. But the newly freed fossil may be incomplete. Restoration involves the use of all the skills at the paleontologist's command, because he must fill in parts that are not only missing, but which he may never have seen. For ex-

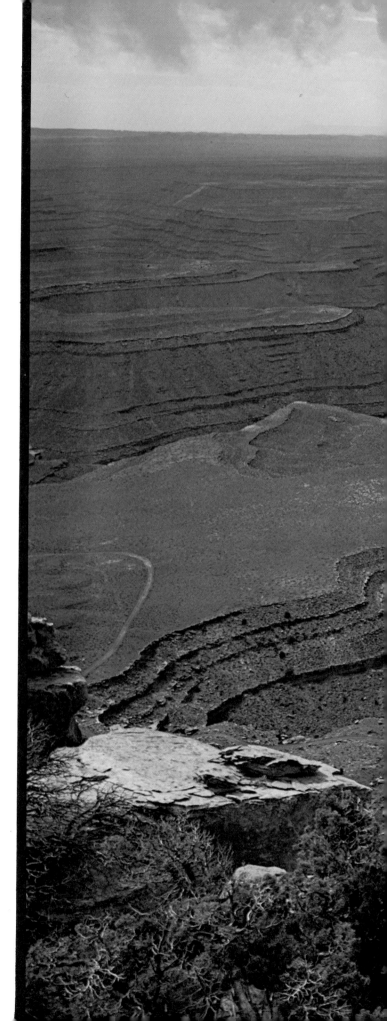

Sea Animals in the Mountains

Paleontologists find fossils of marine creatures high up in the mountains. In fact, many of the highest ranges are composed of layers of sediment originally laid down under the sea. These deposits can be incredibly thick —60,000 feet is not unusual.

Mountain-building forces could tip thick layers of sediment to almost any angle, even vertical. Many of our highest mountains (such as parts of the Rockies) are simply eroded tipped-up sedimentary layers. And it is in these layers that many marine fossils may be found.

A paleontologist can often trace the evolution of past life-forms, in perfect chronological order, down the sides of a mountain. Sometimes the rock layers are overturned, and it takes a great deal of expertise to see the fossil record in the proper perspective.

Certain plants and animals, such as the horse and a small, simple echinoderm named *Microster,* have left almost perfect fossil records. Every branch and twig of their family trees are almost certainly known. Other forms are more secretive. We have only a hairbreadth knowledge of the evolution of the worms, jellyfish, most ancient plants and land animals, and of man. They (and we) do not leave good fossils because bacteria and scavengers ravage the dead before they can be buried and preserved. Soft-bodied creatures are simply compacted with the sea-bottom mud and disappear.

But the stories that have been read along mountainsides, in caves, stream beds, coal mines, and in laboratories have pieced together all that we know about the living past.

Beds of rock. The Grand Canyon shows flat-bedded sediments cut by the Colorado River. The fossils in these beds are in perfect sequence.

Chapter II. Evolution of Evolution

When in 1530 Copernicus wrote in his *Commentariolus* that the sun and not the earth was the center of our universe, man's ego was badly shaken. But Darwin's *Origin of Species* (1859) was infinitely more damaging to man's self-image.

Darwin, a most religious man, explained that his observations of natural life made during his voyages on the *Beagle* reluctantly

---

**"For Darwin subtle variations
within each species
ruled out instant creation."**

---

led him to the unbiblical conclusion that no single flashing moment of creation could account for the great variety of living creatures and plants. During his travels he concluded that subtle and unique variations within each species ruled out instant creation.

In his *Descent of Man,* the result of 20 years of study, Darwin expounded the view that all living organisms come from various lower forms through natural selection and the survival of the fittest. Even the most highly evolved forms, including man, could be traced back to lower organisms whose basic elements we all share. Further back, it would seem that we all owe our lives to the first "genius" molecule of inorganic matter that captured the spark of life. Thus, in part, we are all some 3 billion years old.

Rather than argue who or what created the world and man, let us examine the processes which, after so many eons, produced the countless forms of life on our planet. Darwin was not the first to speculate on evolution. In 600 B.C. the Greek philosopher Thalus thought life originated out of water. Heraclitus wrote that everything living is transposed into new shapes. Aristotle believed

there might be a natural development from plants to plant-animals and finally to man.

During the Middle Ages curious legends were accepted as facts. For generations people believed that geese came from barnacles attached to fruit trees. Some serious scientists were sure that dirty rags and a few grains of wheat could give birth to mice. It was not until the time of the French Revolution, in the early 1790s, however, that the French philosopher Jean Baptiste Lamarck studied seriously the acquired characteristics of animals. Animals, he observed, adapted themselves to various situations like climate and altitude. By constantly using and developing those organs and physical features that were most useful, they changed some of their original features and adapted better to their habitats. The characteristics they acquired in these transformations were then handed down to their offspring. According to Lamarck, this accounted for the variations of species. His views were generally accepted and 70 years later were used to combat Darwin's theories.

Darwin's theories claim that all forms of life are related and all evolved from a common ancestor. Their differences developed over millions of years when they were adapting to their chosen homes, but this infinitely slow form of adaptation was not a simple Lamarckian process. Darwin postulated that those species and individuals in a species that had even a subtle advantage—as small as two or three tiny characteristics—over their fellows survived and multiplied while the less efficient became extinct.

The goose-tree legend. *An early myth, disproven in 1830, claimed that wild geese began life in the sea as gooseneck barnacles which emerged from the water to become adult geese.*

Success through loss. *The moray eel (above) lost its limbs, but not through simple disuse. The ancestors of modern morays were successful because they had smaller fins than their fellows, and their offspring with the smallest fins survived to breed more, and so on, in the normal course of evolution.*

Lamarck

Almost everybody is a Lamarckian until instructed differently. It is very easy to conclude that we have no tail, in contrast to our relative the monkey, because we have lost it through disuse. Or that a giraffe has a long neck because he continually stretched and reached for higher leaves causing it to grow longer. These conclusions seem logical because muscles grow larger through use, and atrophy or shrinking of muscles results from disuse. But well or poorly developed muscles cannot be passed on to the young, and the transfer of characteristics from one generation to the next is the essence of developing new species or different characteristics within the species.

Lamarck's theory was first published in his *Philosophie zoologique* in 1809. He held that an animal's adaptation to the environment was based on use and disuse of body structures and organs. Limbs and organs were fostered or eliminated by the demands of the environment; and the size of limbs and organs was a direct result of the amount of use. By his theory, an eellike ancestor became a limbless eel through its disuse of fins.

If the animal did not use its fins in exploring narrow crevices for food or seeking protection in caves, the fins became smaller. As this life-style continued and fins became of less use, they eventually were lost. The result was eels as we know them today. Lamarck's belief was that whenever such adaptations arose they were inherited and carried from one generation to the next. This meant that a change in an organism, induced by the environment, was transferred in the genetic makeup of the individual.

Although Lamarck's theory seems logical, it has never been substantiated experimentally. We have commonly clipped the tails and ears of dogs for hundreds of generations and yet the young have tails and ears intact, like their ancestors. There are many examples of organs or appendages that are not used for a number of generations and continue in the offspring.

For any adaptation to be transmitted to the next generation a change must take place in the genetic material, and there is no evidence that the use or disuse of body structures can influence the hereditary material. Consequently, scientists generally accept a refinement of Darwin's theory—random mutations are the source of variability, which results in successful adaptations.

Who needs fins? Eels are fish with degenerate fins, but they are enormously successful, and they can often inhabit waters that are too brackish or too dirty for other fish to survive. Wolf eels (below) are of a different lineage than morays, but they too adapted to a limbless life.

Darwin's Finches

The scientific views of creation that prevailed in Charles Darwin's nineteenth-century England were based primarily on a narrow interpretation of the Bible. The Book of Genesis declared: "And God said: Let the waters bring forth abundantly the moving creatures that hath life. . . . Let the earth bring forth living creatures after his kind. . . . Let us make man in our image." Men of knowledge interpreted this to mean a miraculous creation of life and pinpointed the year it occurred—4004 B.C. Darwin came from a religious background and, as a young man, was not ready to challenge this concept of creation.

Receiving his degree from Cambridge, Darwin was taken on as an unpaid naturalist aboard the H.M.S. *Beagle* on her second exploratory-scientific expedition. The ship set sail from Devonport, England, on Dec. 27, 1831. Circumnavigating the globe for five years, Darwin observed things that made him question existing theories on the geology and past history of life on earth.

Birds that made history. *Charles Darwin was struck by the diversity of finches in the Galápagos Islands; many of them (above) are only slightly different from those in South America.*

A bird with tools. *Some Galápagos finches (left) have adapted the most extraordinary technique of using a small stick to reach insects burrowed in trees.*

While crossing the Atlantic from England to South America, Darwin read Volume I of Charles Lyell's *Principles of Geology*. In it, Lyell argued that the earth's continents, plains, and mountains were not shaped by the Flood but rather by the action of wind, rain, earthquakes, volcanoes, and other natural forces and that these remodeling processes were continually at work. Such seemingly logical ideas caused young Darwin to start changing his views on the natural state of the world.

In Charles Darwin's view, life was taking on a new meaning and time new dimensions when, in 1835, the *Beagle* headed westward through the Pacific to the Galápagos Islands. Exploring the dry, volcanic islands, he sought to collect one specimen of each species he observed. What amazed him was that almost every species he found was peculiar to each of the islands. Of the 26 species

of birds he captured, 13 were finches; "a most singular group of finches," Darwin called them. They all bore striking resemblances to each other in the structure of their beaks, in their body form, and in their plummage, yet each was a distinct species. He wrote of the finches that "seeing the gradation and diversity of structure in one small, intimately related group of birds, one might really fancy that from an original paucity of birds in this archipelago, one species had been taken and modified for different ends." The finches gave Darwin insight into what was becoming more and more apparent to him: species were not instantaneously created, but arose from common ancestors.

If the animals and plants on the Galápagos had been very different from those in the rest of the world, Darwin's newly aroused doubts about the theory of a spontaneous creation may have been silenced. However, most creatures there, although distinct varieties, bore a remarkable resemblance to animals and plants on the American continent 600 miles away. Darwin pondered: if new species had been placed on these islands at the time of creation, why did they bear such a resemblance to American forms and why did several of the islands have their own species of tortoise, thrush, or finch. Darwin's answers to these questions resulted in the theory of evolution accepted today—living forms evolve through natural selection and the survival of the fittest.

Darwin arrived back in England in 1836. He published his ideas in two books: *On the Origin of Species* (1859) and *The Descent of Man* (1871). When he began his career, the doctrine of special creation was doubted only by heretics. When he finished, the idea that evolution occurs was accepted by a majority of scientific people. Darwin presented a new way of looking at the universe and all living systems associated with it.

Diving Lizards

The Galápagos Archipelago straddles the equator some 600 miles west of Ecuador. It comprises 14 islands, the largest of which is 75 miles long. When Darwin arrived there in 1835, he was beginning to have doubts about the spontaneous creation of all species. And what he saw there eventually led him to his historic theory.

Reptiles and birds are the two main animal populations of the Galápagos Islands. Insects are scarce, and only two mammalian species (not counting seals) are found—a mouse and a bat. For land animals, getting to these islands meant many weeks floating on a log or a tree branch. Some reptiles, but few mammals, survived this perilous journey. Reptiles have therefore become the dominant land animals on the Galápagos.

Marine iguanas are odd reptilian creatures that inhabit the Galápagos coastline. They swarm over the jagged rocks, snorting vapor from their nostrils when disturbed, appearing much like medieval dragons. Found nowhere else on earth, they look like ferocious beasts from the age of the dinosaurs, but are actually docile, harmless vegetarians that never attack other animals. Marine iguanas are fairly good swimmers and exist wholly on seaweed. Because of swift currents between islands and hungry sharks in deeper water, iguanas rarely venture far from their

Dragons on land and in the sea. The marine (above) and land (right) iguanas are lines of evolution from a common stock. Their structures are similar, but they have very different life habits.

island. As a result, several races have developed with characteristics that differ slightly from island to island.

Inland, the land iguana feeds on leaves and cactus and never mingles with its seagoing relative. Darwin noted that the two species were alike in general structure and in many habits. He later concluded they differ as a result of evolutionary change; each evolved separately in its own environment.

Another reptile indigenous to the Galápagos Archipelago is the giant tortoise whose Spanish name—galápago—gave the islands their name. These huge reptiles weigh up to one quarter of a ton and can live for over 100 years. They are the chief herbivorous grazers of the islands, a niche filled by cattle and sheep on the continent. Indeed, when pirates and whalers introduced sheep, cattle, and donkeys to the islands, these animals outcompeted the native tortoises for food and stripped away the natural cover that protected young tortoises from predation by gulls and hawks. As a result of this and of being killed for food, tortoise populations declined drastically. In 1964 a conservation program was initiated that rid the islands of sheep. Since then, tortoises seem to be holding their own in the fight for survival.

On Pea Plants

As a boy, Gregor Mendel noticed that when his father took cuttings from the fruit trees of the great manor house and grafted them to his own fruit trees, the harvest of fruit and its flavor was enormously improved. Gregor was intrigued by the workings of nature, and when he later became a monk, he devoted himself to natural science. Pondering on the strange but always predictable result of tree graftings, he began his revolutionary experiments working with simple garden peas. It is said that Mendel had an exceptional talent for setting up experiments and was very fortunate to choose garden peas for his work. Peas, in dependable varieties, were available for agricultural purposes and he had no trouble obtaining them. Pea plants could be crossed or self-pollinated with ease and they grew rapidly; attributes that made them very good experimental subjects. However, unknown to Mendel was the fact that pea plants exhibited a minimum number of chromosomal oddities from generation to generation. Since Mendel was unaware that chromosomes even existed, his choice of peas was also a lucky one. Perhaps if he had selected different subjects he would never have hit upon the secrets of inheritance.

Knowing the history of his plants, he first crossed tall plants with dwarf plants. In experiment after experiment, the first-generation results of this pollination were remarkably similar. When Mendel crossed a dwarf variety of pea a foot high with a tall variety six feet high, the hybrids in the next generation were all tall. He next pollinated the hybrids with their own pollen and got plants 75 percent of which were tall and 25 percent of which were dwarf. When he self-pollinated the second generation, all the dwarf plants produced dwarfs, but only one-third of the tall plants continually bred all

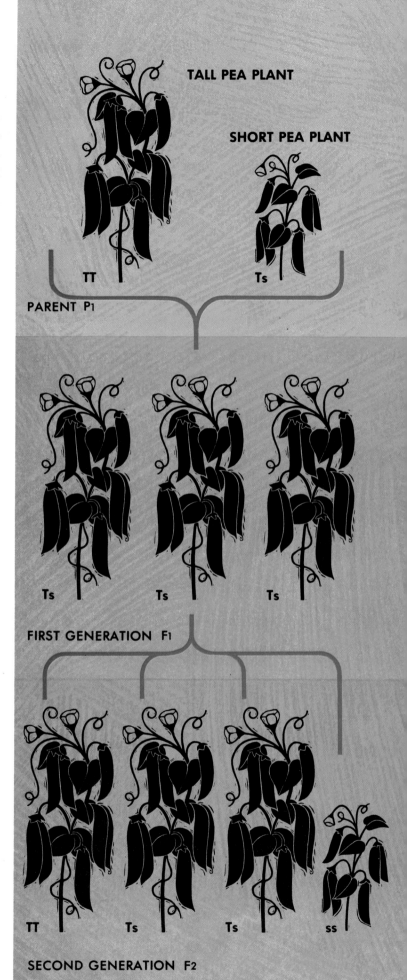

TALL PEA PLANT

SHORT PEA PLANT

TT

Ts

PARENT P1

Ts   Ts   Ts

FIRST GENERATION F1

TT   Ts   Ts   ss

SECOND GENERATION F2

tall plants. The other two-thirds of the tall plants produced third-generation offspring in the ratio of 25 dwarf to 75 tall.

Using many different qualities, Mendel soon found that some characteristics, like dwarfness, could be "masked" and disappear during the reproduction process when mated with the opposite characteristic (such as tallness). In a later generation, however, the masked characteristic, which he called "recessive," would reappear. The masking characteristics he called "dominant." From observing the characteristics of the third generation of plants, Mendel concluded that one-third of the tall plants in the third generation had no dwarf factors (recessive genes) that were being masked and therefore bred all tall plants. The remaining tall plants were masking the dwarf recessive factor, and dwarfness would appear when two recessive factors were combined during fertilization. This led to Mendel's first law: characteristics are controlled by pairs of factors (later named genes and chromosomes), which do not blend during life and which pass into separate cells during the reproductive process, prior to fertilization.

Dominant and Recessive. In these illustrations, tallness dominates shortness. A pea plant can only be short when both recessive genes are present.

In further experiments, Mendel studied plants with two pairs of contrasting characteristics to see how such characteristics would interact in their passage from generation to generation. Using seed form and seed color as subjects, he was able to deduce his second law: a pair of contrasting characteristics may be combined with another pair during the process of reproduction so that there is complete independence of combination among the factors present. In the experiment that lead him to this conclusion, one parent was a purebreeding plant with a round and yellow seed; the other was a purebreeder with a wrinkled and green seed. Plants in the first generation all had round and yellow seeds, indicating that round and yellow seeds were dominant over wrinkled and green ones. In the second generation after self-fertilization, Mendel found that four different sets of characteristics were produced. The ratio was nine : three : three : one (nine plants with round and yellow seeds; three with round and green seeds; three with wrinkled and yellow seeds; and one with wrinkled and green seeds).

It turns out, however, that all characteristics do not behave as perfectly as Mendel's laws suggest. Crossing red snapdragons with white ones produces hybrids of an intermediate pink shade, indicating that there is a greater variety in hereditary factors. Such deviations from the strict dominant-recessive relationship had originally confused Mendel. He never got the opportunity to prove the cause of these inconsistencies but correctly concluded that there may be more than one hereditary unit affecting color and as a result producing a greater possibility of variations. But Mendel's laws when added to Darwin's theories are a great help in explaining the complex hereditary processes that result in the countless variations among all living species on our planet.

Pattern for Life

For centuries it has been the dream of mankind to create life, to make a living creature in the laboratory. Every part of the world is full of stories of wizards and alchemists—most of them evil—who constructed living robots. Unruffled by the morals of these tales, our microbiologists are on the threshold of unlocking some of the most extraordinary secrets of heredity, the chemical processes by which life is duplicated. At some time everyone has wondered what tells our body to start an eye in our face instead of a finger. We take for granted that a child should look like his parents; but on second thought, how does that happen? Why should a dolphin produce a baby dolphin instead of a sea anemone? In short, what is there in every living thing, sponge, animal, flower, fish, or bird, that determines its basic forms and sees to it that they are handed down to the offspring with unmistakable precision? The scientists following up thousands of clues finally hit upon the chromosome as the agent behind this evolutionary process. It was made up of numerous units strung together like beads. These were called genes. When scientists exposed the genes to X rays, they found that a disturbance took place in

Anemone mothers. Infant Epiactis anemones (above) reside at the base of their parents protected by expanded tentacles. The larvae develop within the parent and migrate out through the mouth. After sufficient growth takes place, they will crawl away.

the transmission of the original coded message, and hundreds of mutations, or rearrangements of the genetic material, resulted. Looking further, they discovered that the DNA molecule, or deoxyribonucleic acid, was indeed the director of heredity and is the substance that controls every basic reproductive process of a living organism.

DNA, whose structure resembles a spiraling ladder, is made up of a number of bases attached to a sugar molecule and a phosphate molecule. The sugar and phosphate molecules form the sides of the spiraling ladder, while the rungs of the ladder are made up of paired bases. These bases are actually acting as a code in which three pairs constitute a word (a three-letter word) and the word means one of the amino acids (building blocks of our tissues). Thus the information within DNA is broken down into three-letter words, which when interrogated by the cell tells it how to make a protein, enzyme, organ, or whatever. What happens when a mutation occurs is that one of the letters (a base) of the three-letter word is changed and consequently spells a different word. Most often the word makes the sentence meaningless, which is a detrimental mutation, but once in a while the alteration of a word makes the sentence better and becomes another step toward a more successfully adapted individual. Because this alteration took place in the genetic material, it will be transmitted to the offspring and be an advantage to them also. In essence the constituents of DNA are the same for all plants and animals—only the arrangement of the words (three paired bases on the DNA ladder) differentiates a clam from man.

As biological research goes on, we keep moving closer to the day chance can be eliminated from evolution. This prospect can be frightening, and one only hopes this knowledge will be used to improve, not destroy.

Liberated father. There are no chauvinist pipefish fathers; in fact, males are responsible for all the babysitting. On the pipefish (below) the eggs are retained in a special brooding groove along the belly after release by the female.

The Basis of Evolution

If you observe many generations of laboratory animals (guinea pigs or fruit flies, for example), eventually you will note an individual which is a bit different from its parents. This difference may take almost any form: a short wing on the fly; a notched ear on the guinea pig; a different colored eye on either. This change occurs for no apparent reason, and it may or may not be harmful to the individual. It is a mutation, an "accident" caused by a gene or a set of genes that for some reason has been modified.

This process of mutation is the basic source of variability within populations of animals and plants. Most mutant individuals are not as successful as those that are normal. But an occasional mutation is very much of an advantage and stands a chance of influencing the future of a whole group. Biologists suspect that minor mutations are more useful as a mechanism of population change than are the highly visible ones. Mutated changes are part of the genetic structure of the individual, and they reproduce themselves; this is in contrast to Lamarck's ideas of acquired characteristics where the change

is induced upon the organism and it does not affect the offspring; in fact, our modern understanding of evolution goes a lot farther than Darwin's concept.

If fruit flies are subjected to X rays for a period of time, a series of mutant individuals will be produced among the normal offspring of those flies. Of these mutants, an overwhelming majority will be less fit than their relatives. It's easy to explain why. Natural populations have gone through many generations of mutation, and the subsequent selection of the fittest, to produce the "wild" type that is the most fit. Most of the new mutations will detract from the survival ability of the population and soon disappear. But a small percentage of the mutations will be harmless or possibly beneficial, and these may influence the future of the breed.

There is a second type of mutation, which affects the chromosome rather than the gene. A common way the chromosome mutates is by breaking and recombining in a different pattern. Or parts of a chromosome can crossover with another one.

What causes mutation? No one knows for sure—perhaps it is a failure of the genes to copy themselves properly. There are several known ways to induce mutation, and these are often used by scientists to aid in the study. X rays, certain poisonous gases, some chemicals, and natural radiation such as cosmic rays all cause mutation.

Generally the level of cosmic radiation present on the earth's surface is only high enough to explain about 0.1 percent of the mutations observed in laboratory samples of fruit flies (which reproduce every 17 days, and so are the best experimental animals). There must be some other, still unknown explanation for natural mutations.

But at various times in the earth's history, the magnetic poles have reversed themselves, again for unknown reasons. The consequences of this could be enormous. Without a magnetic field at the moment of reversal, there would be a tremendous increase in the amount of cosmic radiation reaching the earth. The Van Allen belts which now enclose the earth along lines of magnetic force would disappear. If these reversals took any real length of time in the past history of the earth, they might explain some major evolutionary events in the fossil record.

Mutation? *This starfish may be a mutant, or the bifurcation of one limb may show regeneration.*

Chapter III. Survival of the Fittest

The ocean blankets 70 percent of the earth. The highest mountains on land would disappear into the deepest trenches beneath the sea. Habitats in the ocean are many and varied, yet life abounds in all realms of the sea.

Animals that live in the ocean have evolved what seems to be an endless array of adaptations, enabling them to take advantage of conditions unique to their environment. Barnacles and mussels attach themselves to solid rock; fish live among the tentacles of

---

"By 'adaptation' we mean accidental changes that make an animal successful."

---

poisonous jellyfish; crown-of-thorns starfish devour coral polyps; giant whales feed on microscopic plankton; and sargassum fish become invisible to the eye when they swim among the drifting weed.

The fact that a creature is found living in a specific habitat means that it has, through evolutionary processes, become accidentally adapted to its environment. These so-called adaptations can be physiological (changes in body functions and vital processes) and/or morphological (changes in body form and structure). Let us make clear that throughout these books, when we use the rather improper word "adaptation," we mean accidental changes that happen to make such adaptation successful.

Morphological adaptations are usually associated with avoiding predators. Fishes, like tuna and bluefish, are capable of swimming fast and use their speed to keep from being eaten. In turn, some methods of avoidance are passive, such as protective coloration and development of spines. A flounder or stonefish laying on the bottom blends in with its surroundings and is hard to detect. Spines make an animal like a sea urchin or porcupinefish hard to grasp and ingest.

In contrast to passive avoidance, some methods of avoidance are very aggressive. Various weapons, poisons, and even electric shocks are used to ward off potential predators. The tropical doctorfish has, on each side of its tail, a sharp daggerlike spine, which it keeps tucked away under a flap of skin. When threatened, it erects these spines and tries to sideswipe its adversary. The common stingray has a sharp spine at the top of its whiplike tail. If the fish should be disturbed while lying peacefully in the sand, the tail automatically arches upward with the spine becoming buried in the attacker.

Venom is used quite effectively by land creatures and it is also used in the sea. The beautiful tigerfish, scorpionfish, and zebrafish all have venomous glands and can inject poison into an attacking predator through spines that serve as hypodermic needles.

Aquatic creatures possess yet another defensive mechanism: some are capable of delivering electric shocks. The most prodigious of these creatures is the electric eel, found in South American waters. This animal can deliver a charge of 550 volts and 1000 watts —strong enough to kill some predators and to jolt even the largest attackers.

Chance mutations are not always successful. Throughout the history of life on earth vast numbers of creatures that could no longer meet the demands of an everchanging environment have become extinct.

A roving eye. The eyes of most flatfish have adapted to a bottom-dwelling life by having the downward one migrate up to join its mate.

Incessant Competition

There is only so much food and so much space in the sea, and in the more desirable locations there are usually several organisms that would like to exploit these resources.

There are other things to compete for. Sunlight is necessary for photosynthetic plants and animals and for those which live off them. The shaded will die. Access to nutrient-laden currents can mean the difference between life and death. And the young of one's kind must have a place to grow up.

Almost all interactions between living beings are involved with some form of competition. The exceptions are mutualism, commensalism, and parasitism. These three interactions are sophisticated arrangements whereby two or more organisms can occupy the same or a

Competition for space. Here living space is at a premium, and the rock substrate (above) is completely covered with life. The yellow sponge surrounds a solitary coral and seems to be overgrowing the pink coralline algae.

close living space at the same time. In mutualism, each benefits from the relationship. Commensal relationships are benign; one or more gain, none lose. In parasitism one lives off the other, but a prudent parasite does not kill its host or it too usually dies.

The form of competition that seems to communicate the feeling of stability, which the natural world always establishes, may be termed equilibrium competition. Most organisms live in a stable community which evolves as a unit. Personnel in the community may change a bit, but its overall structure remains as long as the environment is

unchanged. Animals and plants are usually zoned within their communities, and communities themselves are zoned.

The classic example of zoned animals and plants is in the North Atlantic nearshore intertidal environment. Mussels of the genus *Mytilus* (the common edible mussel) and barnacles of the genus *Chthamalus* can withstand long periods of exposure to air and drying. They occupy the highest reaches of the intertidal zone and the higher portions of pilings. The horse mussel *Modiolus*, and the barnacle *Balinus* need more submergence and they are lower on the pilings and nearer the low-tide mark. The soft-shelled clam, *Mya*, can withstand the longest period of time out of water, buried under the surface, and it can be found at the highest intertidal. *Mercenaria*, the quahog clam, and *Polinices*, the moon snail, must remain underwater. They may try to invade each other's territory, but will be driven back by conditions that better suit another.

Parasites for space. The yellow polyps (above), unable to secrete their own supporting structure, are overgrowing the orange gorgonian and outcompeting it for its own skeleton. Instead of being parasites for food, these polyps may be considered parasites by taking up living space at the host's expense.

Silent war. Colonial ascidians surround a small patch of pink coralline algae (below). An obvious zone of conflict marks the boundary of each.

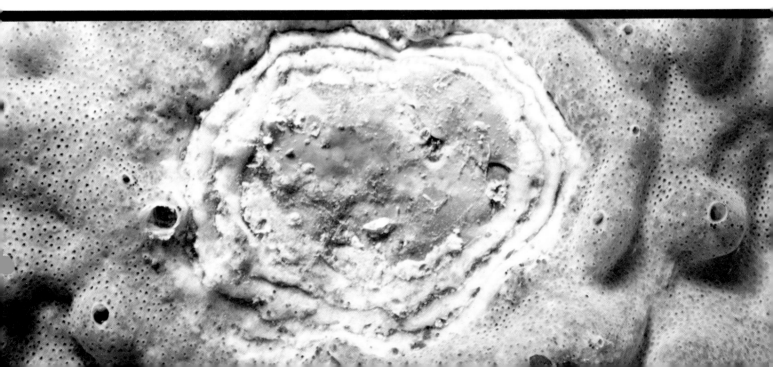

The Fight for Life

The struggle of life reaches down to the individual. Every living organism has its natural enemies—although in some cases these may be a short food supply or a harsh environment. If it were not so, the seas would teem with solid-packed masses of flesh, and then all would die.

But there are usually a few creatures who specialize in living off the bodies of a particular plant or animal, and to ward off the ad-

Diversionary tactics. A goby consumes the internal organs ejected by a sea cucumber (above). As a defensive maneuver, the sea cucumber may preserve itself by giving up a portion of its body.

vances of these special predators, almost all animals evolve a means of defense.

Some of these adaptations can be bizarre. The simplest are perhaps the least obvious. If a fish is big, only larger predators will usually bother it. Or it may be small enough to hide where its enemies can't follow. Thus size becomes perhaps one of the first defenses. Schooling behavior provides the proverbial "safety in numbers," both by having one's fellows help in the counterattack and by increasing the number of bodies around so that the predator will be full by the time he gets to a specific individual.

Teeth, shells, and sharp spines play an obvious role in defense, as do poison, aggressive behavior (a good offense may be the best defense), and speed of flight. Sometimes a lucky creature will have a working combination of techniques at its disposal. Some fish swell up, when under attack or stress, by swallowing air or water. The porcupinefish combines this with spines and becomes a ball of prickles. And in many of the categories of living organisms are forms which just plain taste bad.

One of the curious cases of convergent evolution is the development, in many different groups, of electric organs. The paleozoic ostracoderms were the first, and today there are the electric eel, torpedo ray, electric catfish, stargazers, and a number of other electric fish. Electricity is used not only in defense but as an aid to food gathering—to stun prey into submission.

And then there is the unattractive, but often effective technique of ejecting part of one's

self or some body fluid to either repel an intruder or to confuse him. The squid's ink is a well-known example. Some worms release part of their body, perhaps to satisfy the predator enough to permit escape. The sea cucumber does a most efficient job of this sort of defense. It can extrude sticky, sometimes poisonous threads, or it can evicerate or eject some of its digestive tract for a predator to eat. As long as there is competition, there will be defenses that permit survival.

Sticky tubules. The mass of cuvarian tubules ejected by this sea cucumber (above and below) presents an unappetizing mouthful to a predator. In some species the sticky strands are poisonous.

Incognito

Lying on the nearshore sea bottom is a layer of stones and sand. But wait—if one steps on this particular little patch of sand, it swims away. It was, of course, a flounder—nature's most artful dodger.

When sunlight penetrates into the sea, it creates shadows below anything that blocks the light. If a uniformly colored fish were swimming in the bright photic zone, it would appear to have a light, highly visible top-surface and a dark undersurface. So, many open water fish have a light underside and a dark top, which makes them appear evenly colored in sunlight.

Curiously, certain African catfish are camouflaged in the reverse way (light above, dark below)—and they swim on their backs!

There are many types of fish that can change their colors. The way this adaptation is achieved is usually through the use of specialized pigment cells called chromatophores. These cells have branching projections into which the pigment of that particular chromatophore may be spread. The pigment can be brown, yellow, orange, or white, depending upon which chemical the fish has adapted to its needs. When the pigment spreads through the chromatophore, the fish is camouflaged over the small area served by that cell. When not needed, the pigment collects into an almost invisible spot.

The protection offered by camouflage is not perfect, but it works well enough for a sufficient number of each species to survive and reproduce. Camouflage evolves because the hardest to find may be the last eaten, and so their offspring guide the future of their kind.

*A mouthful of teeth hidden in the sand. The well-camouflaged **goosefish** (below) lies in wait on the sandy bottom. Any prey which approaches too close is sucked into its gaping mouth and devoured.*

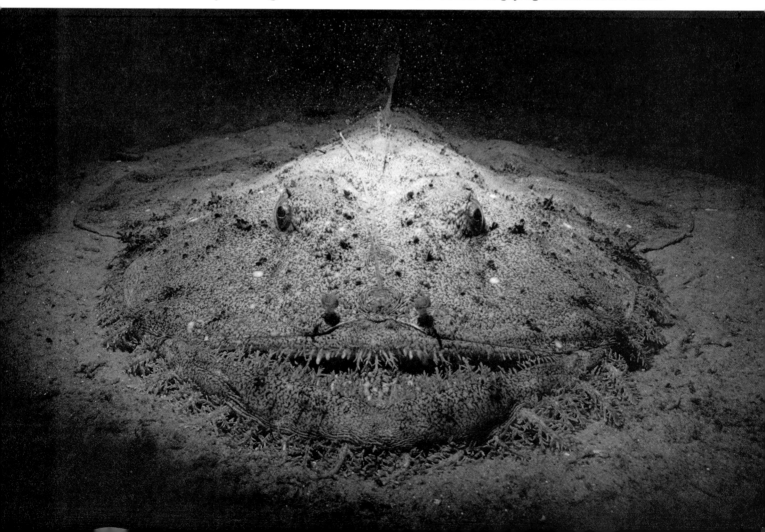

Great Pretenders

Imitation is the sincerest form of flattery—
so the pundits say. It can also be a good
recipe for survival. We might consider mimicry to be a sophisticated means of camouflage, except that in mimicry one doesn't
necessarily want to be hidden, just mistaken
for something else.

If you sieve some water from among a stand
of eel grass in the North Atlantic nearshore
region, you will probably have several pipefish in your net. Put them back please, but
consider where they were hiding. They are
right there in front of your eyes, mimicking
the blades of eel grass.

Diving in the Sargasso Sea, one may see a
certain type of seahorse (*Phyllopteryx*),
but one must look carefully because they
possess appendages and colors that blend in
perfectly with the sargassum itself.

Swimming seaweed (above). The sargassum fish
(Histrio histrio) *mimics the sargassum itself with
branched appendages and a precise color match.*

In some cases of mimicry, animals look like
more dangerous forms. Certain eels mimic
the poisonous sea snakes so well that a
trained scientist usually cannot tell the difference if both are in the water.

Or an animal can imitate a more gentle creature. A predatory blenny mimics the harmless, and in fact symbiotically useful, wrasse
of the genus *Labroides*. The wrasse cleans
parasites off other fish, rendering a service
and simultaneously feeding itself. But the
blenny wishes only to rip pieces off the fish
that are seeking the wrasse's assistance.

The mimic is rarer than the mimicked—
otherwise the predators and/or prey would
be too suspicious for anyone to benefit.

The Joys of Degeneracy

There is a social stigma associated with the concept of degeneracy, but all of us have some degenerate organs in our bodies. The appendix comes quickly to mind.

It is unwise in nature to retain an organ which serves no function. The blood supply usually must nourish it, and the developing germ plasm in the embryo must further divide to produce it. The energy available in an organism must be spent wisely, or there may not be enough for the vital needs of the necessary parts. If an unused part does not develop properly, there is no loss, it becomes degenerate and it is eventually eliminated.

Some fish are degenerate with respect to so many parts that the result can be called overall degeneracy. The male anglerfish found in the deep sea leads a parasitic life permanently attached to the much larger female. It is reduced to being simply a set of sex organs and a nutrient extractor totally dependent on the female's system.

Among the molluscs there are very fine examples of degeneracy. The shipworms have only a rudimentary pair of shells attached near the head. Nudibranchs, as the name implies, have lost almost all traces of their shells. Some clams have lost their shells, which makes them seem very unclamlike.

But a degenerate organism is often highly successful, as any gardener, who has watched his tomatoes being overrun by slugs which lack a shell, can attest.

Naked clam. *The weird-looking animal shown below is a clam whose shells have become degenerate and lie within its tissues.*

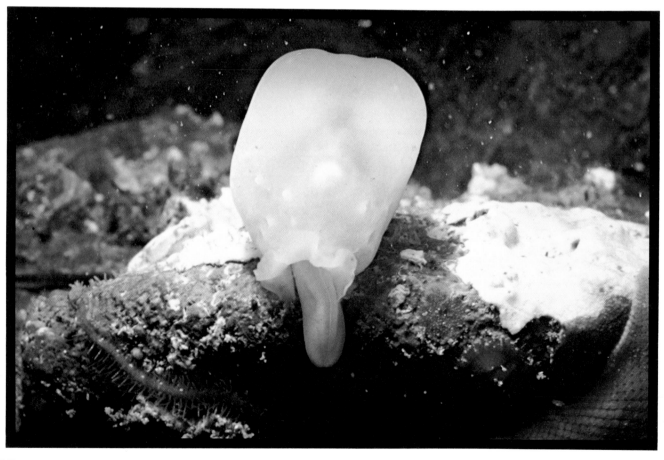

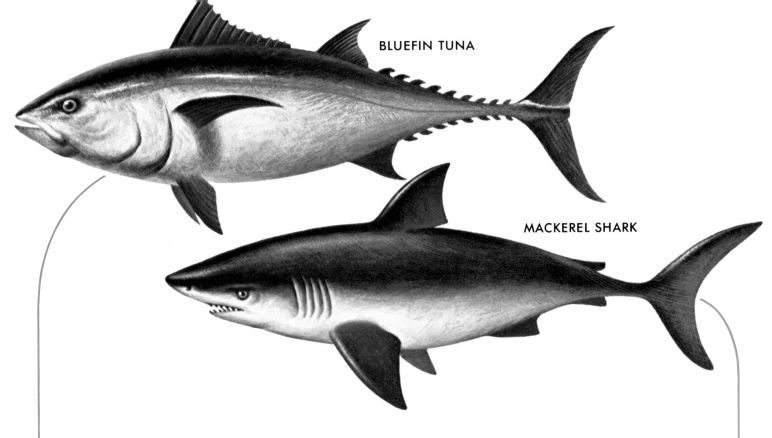

BLUEFIN TUNA

MACKEREL SHARK

Convergence

When animals that are not closely related develop under similar conditions, through natural selection they may exhibit superficial similarities. This phenomenon is known as convergent evolution.

A good example of convergence is the similarities between two distantly related sea forms, the tunas and isurid sharks, which include the makos, mackerel sharks, and great whites. Both have similar color patterns, fin arrangements, and streamlined bodies. Their gills are large; muscles used in locomotion are well developed; and the circulatory system has developed in such a way as to make them warm-blooded. These convergences reflect the way these fishes live: both

are restless, far-ranging wanderers capable of great bursts of speed.

Being warm-blooded gives these fish an advantage over cold-blooded forms. By increasing their body temperature, they have increased the rate at which their muscles can contract and relax. (The rate of the chemical reactions involved is dependent upon temperature; therefore the higher the temperature the faster the reaction.) It has been calculated that for a 10° C. rise in body temperature, these fish can get three times as much power from a given set of muscles. When ambient temperatures drop, fish become sluggish because their chemical reactions have slowed down. However, the tunas and isurid sharks can still cruise the waters in a seemingly effortless fashion.

TERTIARY

CRETACEOUS

JURASSIC

TRIASSIC

PERMIAN

CARBONIFEROUS

DEVONIAN

Divergence

In divergent evolution closely related forms evolve differences in body structure and function which eventually lead to the formation of a new species. This process, which occurs through natural selection, can be thought of as the opposite of convergent evolution.

Perhaps the most diverse group of animals in the sea are the Crustacea; over 25,000 species have been identified. Because they are so diverse and because they belong to the phylum Arthropoda, as do the insects, crustaceans have often been called the "insects of the sea." Most are marine, yet some do inhabit freshwater lakes and streams. A few even live on land, as their gills have been modified in ways that do not require continual wetting to be effective. Although most crustaceans can be found in the lighted portions of the sea, walking, creeping, or swimming about, others burrow in the bottom and some even inhabit the deepest part of the ocean, migrating to the surface at night or crawling on the bottom.

Crustaceans come in assorted sizes, shapes, and colors and with a variety of life-styles. Barnacles spend their entire adult lives attached firmly to rocks or pilings; only their nauplius larvae are free-swimming. A relative of barnacles, *Sacculina*, is a parasite that infests crabs, sending rootlike processes throughout the host's body.

Many crustaceans are microscopic in size. Copepods are microscopic crustaceans that make up the bulk of the zooplankton in the

Bulk. *The stone crab (below) is a massive, slow-moving crustacean which depends on its size and armor to keep enemies away.*

oceans of the world. They are an important part of the ocean food chain and essential in the diet of fish larvae and some adult fish. Some copepods are parasites and can be found attached to fish, drawing nourishment from the fish's blood and lymph.

Shrimp are well-known crustaceans and have adapted to a wide range of habitats, from sandy tidal flats to coral reefs. A closely related form is the lobster. Both are commercially important resources. Also related to the lobsters and shrimp are the crabs, a specific group of crustaceans that exhibit a wide range of evolutionary divergences. Some, like *Cancer* (the rock crab), have legs adapted for running over the bottom. This is in contrast to the American blue-claw crab, whose fifth pair of legs has been modified into paddlelike structures for swimming. Spider crabs, in turn, have long spindly legs. The giant of all crustaceans is the Japanese spider crab. Found in deep waters offshore, it reaches a length of 11 feet from claw to claw. In contrast are the tropical ghost crabs that measure about two inches wide. They are referred to as the "rabbits of the crustaceans," for they are often seen racing over the beach away from enemies.

Some crabs inhabit the cold waters of Alaska, some the deep ocean floor, and others land. All crustaceans however arose from the same primitive stock many millions of years ago and through the phenomenon of divergent evolution have radiated out to fill the innumerable habitats they occupy today.

Lightweight. Unlike the heavy shelled crabs, the arrow crab (below) successfully avoids being eaten with a delicate framework.

Chapter IV. Evolution and Reproduction

When the right combination of chemicals produced a living organism, it had to be able to duplicate itself, or the great achievement of life would not have been perpetuated. Reproduction then was the vehicle through which evolution did its work. Recombination and reshuffling of genetic material, over billions of years, has taken life from one-celled protozoans to man.

Asexual reproduction is the most primitive mode of self-duplication. It occurs in a number of ways. Binary fission is a method com-

---

"Reproduction is the vehicle through which evolution took place."

---

mon to unicellular organisms. Chromosomal material, as well as all cellular components, are duplicated. The protoplasm divides and the cell splits in two, with each portion receiving exactly half the genetic material and about half of the other material.

Another form of asexual reproduction in simple multicellular animals is budding, a process where a miniature of the adult grows attached to the parent's body. Eventually, the developing bud drops off and takes up an independent existence.

Sexual reproduction is a process wherein genetic material is interchanged between individuals. This was a crucial step forward because exchanges of genetic material allowed for greater genetic variation in organisms.

An early group which reproduces almost exclusively by sexual means were the fish. Eggs and sperm could be released into the water where fertilization and subsequent development could take place. However, such a method produces high mortality for eggs, so that the only fishes that survived

were those capable of releasing great quantities of roe. For example, a female cod may release as many as nine million eggs during one spawning spasm.

As life moved to land, reproductive patterns did not change drastically at first. Amphibians, the first land creatures, still returned to water to breed, as they generally do today. Frogs even have a tadpole stage that must live out its life in water.

Reptiles, the next group of animals to arrive on the scene, broke away from a dependence upon water by developing an egg with a protective shell. Surrounding the embryo within the porous shell was a membrane, the amnion, that formed a liquid-filled cavity. This was, in essence, a substitute for the external aquatic environment needed by earlier amphibians. Other membranes that developed included the allantois, which served as a medium for gas exchange through the shell; the yolk sac, which had a rich supply of food material; and the chorion, which lined the inside of the shell. This pattern was copied by birds, and many of the features are still seen in the wrappings of human embryos.

What now appears to be the latest stage in the evolution of reproduction is that reached by higher mammals: a placental connection between embryo and mother. Here, there is no shell protecting the egg and development is within the mother. The chorion comes into contact with maternal tissue, forming a placenta through which nutrients and oxygen pass and waste products are removed.

A fair exchange. Animals which normally reproduce asexually, such as Paramecium (right), follow the instinctive need to get together and exchange genetic material to increase future variability.

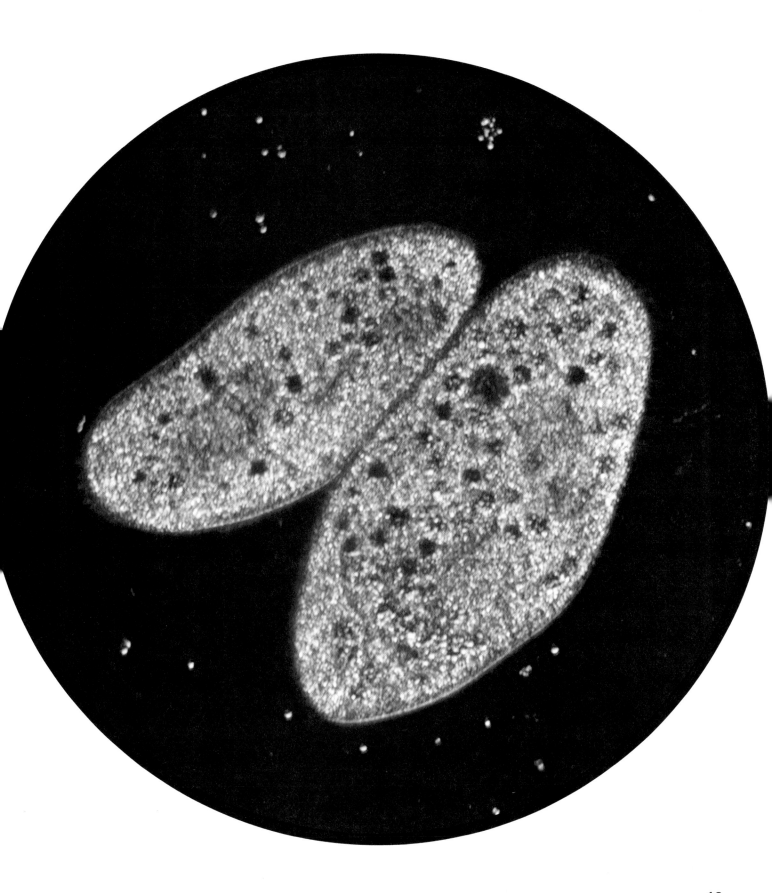

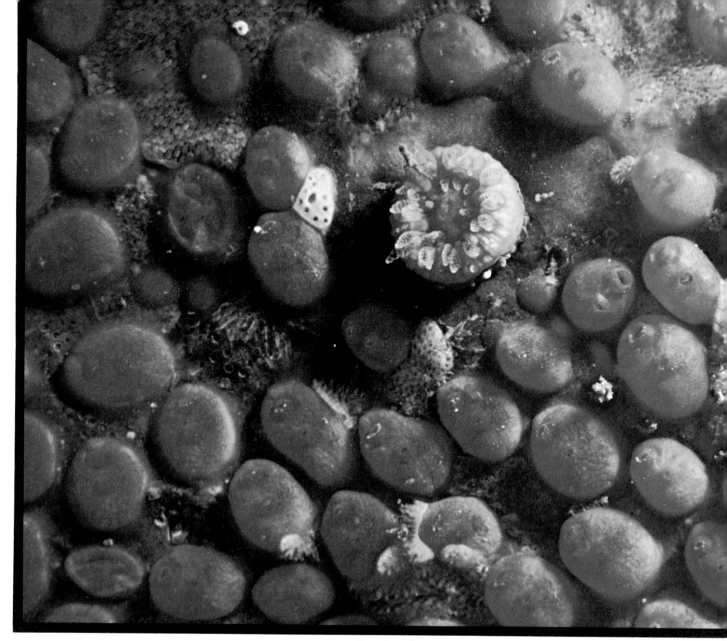

From One-Many

Reproduction is one of the basic drives of any living system. It motivates both amoeba and man. Any adult organism is essentially a mechanism capable of keeping itself functioning until such a time that it can contribute to the continuation of its lineage. When it has accomplished this function, it begins to deteriorate and eventually die, removing itself from competition with its progeny for food and space.

For all creatures, plants and animals alike, whose existence depends upon the continual production of offspring, asexual reproduc-

tion has become a way of life. For organisms that sit firmly attached to the bottom, it precludes the necessity to find a mate. Asexual reproduction does not depend upon the sometimes haphazard meeting of a sperm and egg. This is important for organisms who live isolated existences—whose gametes might never reach those of a partner. For a sea squirt or sea anemone to successfully perpetuate its kind, all it has to do is divide itself in two.

Asexual reproduction is a trait common to lower forms of life. Almost all fish and amphibians and certainly all reptiles, birds, and mammals have abandoned this mode of rep-

Budding. These sea squirts (above) are reproducing asexually, as the young develop from thin extensions of the parent's tissues.

lication for sexual reproduction. The greater evolutionary advances these groups have made over the annelids or cnidarians stem, no doubt, from the fact that every time sardines, whales, penguins, turtles, or humans reproduce sexually, genetic material is exchanged among individuals. This results in an incalculable degree of genetic variation above that of asexually reproducing forms. When a sea squirt buds off a new individual, the offspring's genetic makeup is practically identical to its parent's. Change can come only through mutation. On the other hand, a human baby receives genetic material from two sources and is a unique individual. The odds are infinitesimally small that its parents, or any other two people, will ever produce an offspring identical to it.

Some lower forms of life, while they reproduce asexually, also can produce progeny by sexual means. This gives them the best of two worlds. It allows them to produce the individuals without the presence of a mate, while also giving them a mechanism for genetic variation. This is necessary if they are to readily adapt, through natural selection, to changes in their environment.

45

Gifts from Two Parents

When two individuals produce offspring, they bestow a priceless gift on their progeny. This gift goes beyond the gift of life itself. It is the chance to be different; or more accurately it is the almost certain necessity that the offspring will be different.

The genes of even the simplest sexually reproducing animal or plant are so complex that the chances of repetition of the genetic code are almost nil. In humans, this repetition occurs only in identical twins, which are the result of a fertilized egg dividing in half. This variation inherent in sexually reproducing organisms is one of the most effective

Baby adults. *These baby surf perch, or Embiotocids (below), are born alive and are sexually mature at birth. Within a few days they will mate in dense swarms of baby adults.*

Future shark. *Unlike many sharks which derive nourishment from their yolk sacs, these babies (opposite page), have placentalike connections through which they feed directly off the mother.*

tools of evolution. A variable species can better cope with a changing environment than can a nonvariable species. The presence of a single slightly better-adapted individual can provide the basis for a whole new, and probably more successful, species.

Other properties of the gene are exploited in sexual reproduction. Groups of characteristics tend to be inherited together because they are "linked" as genes on a single chromosome. This linkage alters the simple Mendelian principles significantly and produces complicated interactions between new and existing characteristics in an organism.

Some of these linked genes are sex-linked. That is, they occur on the X and Y sex chromosomes and are usually expressed (appear) in one or the other sex. A tendency toward hemophilia in the royal families of several European nations during the last century is a striking example—only males can be hemophiliacs. Baldness and color blindness are other common sex-linked characteristics in man.

Genes can cross-over between chromosomes, and by this method radically alter the phenotype (appearance) of their host.

Farmers and "fish-farmers" reap the benefits of sexual reproduction in their daily work. They have produced strains of pest-resistant crops, new and desirable types of livestock, crops, and fish but a price has, in some cases, been paid. In selecting those attributes by inbreeding, some groups have become less hardy. For example, some inbred animals are highstrung or are less resistant to some diseases. There may not be any one specific problem, but the group may lack hybrid vigor. This vigor is evident when two different strains are crossed and produce offspring that are bigger, stronger, or better at something than their parents. The exact reasons are not known, but it traces directly to the increase in variability introduced by sexual reproduction. In a wild population, there is some degree of interbreeding and therefore some heterosis ("hybrid vigor"). It is only when artificial circumstances prevent this natural attribute from being exploited that a large number of weak or deformed individuals are produced.

The schools of fish, pods of whales, swarms of copepods and krill, and the general bounties of the vast resources of higher-life-forms owe most of their diversity and success to the simple act of mating.

Shark embryo. *The catshark (above) develops on its own, consuming its yolk sac as it grows.*

The Human Fish

Life evolved in water, probably in the sea. And the sea life slowly increased its complexity and braved the land. In the process gills were succeeded by lungs, and each land creature retained a salt solution within its body. Today man retains vestiges that allude to his aquatic ancestry.

As a broad schematic overview of the course of evolution, this generalization impressed the German biologist Ernst Haeckel. Actually Fritz Müller came up with the idea, but Haeckel is generally credited with formalizing and popularizing the notion that an animal's embryonic development follows its evolution. The study of the development of the unborn is called embryology and the development process is called ontogeny. At some point in the development of birds, reptiles, and mammals (including humans), the embryo—the developing unborn animal—has nonfunctioning gills. Unborn snakes develop limbs and then lose them. We develop from a fishlike fetus, which gradually loses its gills, develops legs, and becomes a reptile. The fetal human heart has two chambers at first, which "evolve" into the mammalian four-chambered heart. All mammals go through this process.

The process of evolving higher and higher forms of life is called *phylogeny,* and now the meaning of Haeckel's cryptic phrase becomes clear. He suggested that in the course of development from the fertilized egg to the completed infant, an animal goes through many of the stages of evolution that the whole of its race has done before it.

It was an exciting concept. The evolution of animals could be traced from the fetus of a higher form. Ancestry could be studied within the single individual. This idea gained great support and is still believed by many people, some of them biologists.

But problems arose from this idea. Scientists noted that there were two general groups of features that appear in the development of individuals and animal groups—generalized and specialized features. The aspects of phylogeny or primitive structures that were usually "recapitulated" by the developing embryos were the general ones.

The human embryo (above) develops primitive characteristics which it loses before birth.

Sometimes organs do not develop in the embryo in the same chronological order as they have been shown to develop in the evolutionary history of the species. In the earliest fishes, teeth appeared before the development of the tongue. In mammalian embryogeny the tongue comes first. There are countless other exceptions. But Haeckel was partly right. Our modern approach to "Haeckel's law" is summarized by the enigmatic phrase "ontogeny recapitulates phylogeny." The mammal develops gill clefts for the reasons that the fish embryo does—natural selection has not condemned this as a reason for unfitness. The genes for gills occurred before and they are still there.

And although the study of the embryo, influenced by Haeckel and his fellows, has vastly increased our understanding of life, we are not bound to reevolve with each new individual born. It just seems that we do.

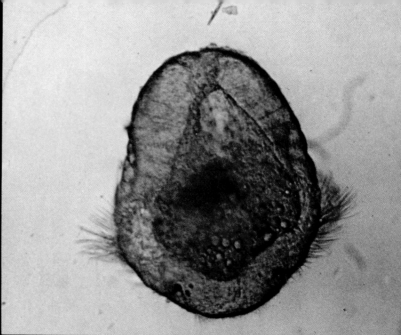

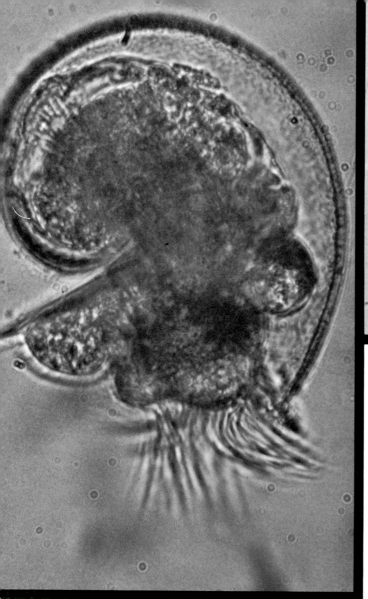

Babies. *The similarity of the veliger larva of the common periwinkle* Littorina *(left) and the trochophore larva of the annelid* Notomastus *(above) shows the relationship between their phyla.*

Larval Links

As animals have developed, adapted, and diverged from one another and have formed new species, they have often retained links with their past. Total abandonment of all ancestral characteristics is rare. Because the larval stage is one of the most important and in many ways one of the most unique periods of an animal's life, it appears to be more resistant to change than other less essential aspects. In general, groups of animals can be separated or linked by the characteristics of their larvae, although there are many individual larval adaptations which help to insure the survival of the individual.

The anemones and jellyfish are a group of simple multicellular animals whose relationship to protozoans can be inferred from their larvae. The planula larvae of this group consists of a free-swimming, ciliated ball of cells. This is not unlike some of the colonial protozoans, which possess some division of labor between cells modified for nutrition, reproduction, and locomotion. These locomotor cells often possess flagella or cilia. To make an anemone or jellyfish from a colony of protozoans or planula larva, one side of the ball of cells must simply be pushed inward forming a double layer surrounding a chamber with a single opening. In a jellyfish the outer layer would constitute the ectoderm, and the endoderm would surround the indented digestive cavity whose opening would be the mouth. The body form of the most simple flatworms (Platyhelminthes) suggests that they may share some affinity with this primitive planula larval form.

Another very interesting larval form is the trochophore larva. It is somewhat rounded and in the shape of a compressed diamond.

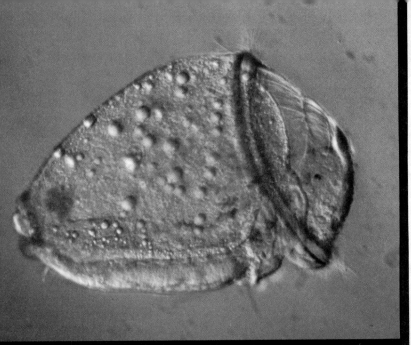

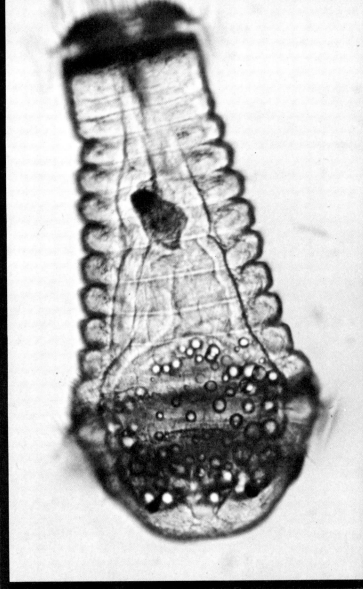

Common ancestor. The trochophore larva (right and above) is the link between several of the most important invertebrate groups, linking clams, annelid worms, and even bryozoans—the moss animals.

There is a U-shaped gut, which extends from one extreme edge to the most ventral portion of the body. A band of cilia surrounds the larva at the equator, and another region near the anus may also possess cilia. In addition to the gut, trochophores contain a nervous system, sensors, and a kidneylike system. This bilaterally symmetrical larval type is seen in a number of the invertebrates, and serves as a basic link between annelids (such as polychaete worms) and molluscs (clams, snails, and the like). In the molluscs the larval form is termed a veliger larva but basically it is of the trochophore body plan. In addition the trochophore type larva indicates a common ancestry between the bryozoans (mosslike animals) and phoronids (primitive wormlike creatures). The arthropods have incredibly complex varieties of larval development among their almost one million species. The free-swimming crustacean nauplius larva is perhaps the most characteristic form.

One of our main reasons for placing echinoderms (starfish and urchins) on the line leading to fish is the similarity of the echinoderm larva to the tornaria larva of the acorn worm, a primitive chordate. The free-swimming larva of echinoderms is very different from the trochophore larva of molluscs and annelids; it is more flattened and has looped bands of cilia for locomotion. Even though most echinoderms are radially symmetrical, the larvae are bilaterally oriented, indicating an ancestry with similar symmetry. This shows that the echinoderms are far removed from the annelid-mollusc line of evolution. Thus the similarity between the starfish and acorn worm larvae lead us to conclude that man is more closely related to starfish than to the highly intelligent octopus.

Chapter V. Experiments in Evolution

As the natural environment changes, creatures that live in it must also change. We have seen that evolutionary processes are gradually, producing new forms of life over long periods of time. In nature, experiments are constantly carried out, producing a never-ending array of strange, bizarre, and sometimes grotesque creatures. As odd as some animals may seem to us, their features usually represent special capabilities that

---

"Countless genetic experiments produce a never-ending array of very strange creatures."

---

have enabled them to survive in the constant struggle to obtain food, reproduce, and thwart enemies.

Among the invertebrates there are many strange and monstrous creatures. Common jellyfish, inhabitants of coastal waters around the world, are usually feared by swimmers, and well they should be. The largest jellyfish known are the mammoth blue-and-orange cyanes of the North Atlantic which grow up to 12 feet in diameter with tentacles over 100 feet long.

A well-documented monstrous invertebrate is the giant squid. This beast reaches 50 feet in length with suckers eight inches in diameter. This animal is the common diet of the sperm whale, which often bears the scars of battle. One huge sperm whale examined by scientists had clearly identifiable sucker marks on its skin that measured 18 inches in diameter. The researchers estimated the squid that inflicted those wounds must have been about 200 feet long.

A relative of the squid is the octopus. One species that occurs in the Pacific is the largest commonly known octopus, reaching a weight of 125 pounds and a length of 20 feet from tip of one arm to the tip of the opposite arm. However, in 1896 the remains of some large creature was washed ashore on the beach off St. Augustine, Florida. Scientists studying it were undecided as to its nature; some said squid or octopus, others said it was part of a whale. Samples of the beast were saved, and they found their way to the Smithsonian Institute. A few years ago a scientist from Miami studied the preserved tissue and concluded the monster was indeed an octopus. From original measurements made on the beast, its length was estimated at 200 feet from arm tip to arm tip.

Vertebrates in the sea have also been experimented upon by nature, and some strange and odd creatures are the result. Perhaps the largest bony fish in the sea is the ocean sunfish. Covered with a thick leathery skin, it seems to be all head and no body. A specimen caught in the Pacific Ocean off the coast of California measured 11 feet in diameter and weighed one ton. The sunfish occasionally comes to the surface where it basks in the sun. This large creature feeds on small planktonic organisms including jellyfish.

Experimentation by nature goes on almost continuously. Somewhere in the sea at this moment one or more variants of a species are being born, and those that survive stand a good chance of being the parents of new species, some we might call monsters.

Fish nightmare. Awesome as it appears to human eyes, the hagfish (right) is a real threat to other fish. A descendant of the jawless ostracoderms, the hagfish makes a living by sucking the life juices from haddock, cod, or similar fish. Hagfish bore into the living fish using rasplike teeth and then burrow all the way inside the fish, often leaving little more than a living skeleton for other predators to attack.

Blondes and Redheads

The variation in human populations is perfectly obvious to us because we deal with it every day. We recognize our friends (and enemies) by their characteristics. A mother has no trouble recognizing her baby's cry. But it is a curious fact that people of one racial type sometimes cannot see the variation quite as easily in another. The result is phrases like "all whites, blacks, or Chinese look the same." They do not; it is only that the observer has not trained his perception to catch variations in the populations.

As humans, we often miss the variation in the animals we observe. Perhaps our pet dog looks different from other people's, but we can't see the variety among clams. The differences are there, however.

All the genetic mechanisms of mutation, gene flow, selection, and adaptation contribute to the variability of natural populations. Some populations are generally more vari-

The same but different. *These wrasses are members of the same species. Their colors exemplify the variations that can exist within a population.*

Galápagos wrasses. *Like so many animals of the Galápagos Islands, these fish demonstrate how evolution produces variations on a theme.*

able than others. One of the reasons for this may deal with basic survival and evolution.

It is a general rule that a form with a high degree of specialization has lost most of its potential to evolve into something quite different. When searching the fossil record for ancestors of a new type of animal, we look at the primitive, generalized possibilities first. Evolution is usually nonreversible.

There is a give-and-take set of advantages to being generalized or specialized. It's good to be well adapted to your ecological niche when the niche is present, but safer not to be overspecialized when the conditions change.

Many fish show a considerable range in their coloration. This can be considered evidence of variability within the population, or it can be evidence that there is more than one population. The scientists who are concerned with putting animals in categories—the taxonomists—are usually in a continuous dither about the concept of the word "species." When is a variant a new species?

Sea Clowns

When the batfish is hungry, it sends out its tackle, via a sort of pistonlike mechanism, and vibrates it for a while to lure in a naive fish. This vibration is in only one direction; some fish of the same species are "righties," some are "lefties."

As a clown, the batfish hops or waddles across the bottom. No dignified swimming for it, it may occasionally look as if it is desperately trying to learn how to swim and gets by for a few strokes. By chance, any structure on the batfish that might look somewhat normal has been altered. The pectoral fins are enlarged to the point where they project forward and outward, looking like a frog's front legs. Underneath the clumsy body, the pelvic fins too serve as walking legs. Still it cannot walk well.

In general almost anyone can laugh at a batfish, except perhaps for the prey that are occasionally attracted by its lazy fishing techniques and vibrating bait.

Fisherman. The batfish (below) fishes with the aid of the "tackle" that sticks out from under its head. It doen't seem exceptionally good at anything, but it does enough well enough.

The Walking Bush

That pretty plant growing along the subtidal zone in the North Atlantic sometimes gets up and walks away on its branches. It is not a plant, of course, but a basket star.

In the basket star a way of feeding has evolved unlike that of most other starfish. Instead of extending its stomach out over its prey, it carries the food to its stomach with its multibranched arms. Basically it functions as a filter feeder; it extends its arms at night, uncoiling all the tendrils and ensnaring any small animals that can be caught. When food has been trapped, the arm wilts and brings it to the mouth. By day it wilts into a mass of arms; by night it feeds.

The number of branches on a single basket star can exceed 90,000. They all eventually join toward the central disk into the customary five arms of most starfish. The common Atlantic genus, *Gorgonocephalus*, may be two feet across, from tip to tip; the body is about four inches across.

Basket star (below). A living bush that grows, wilts, and walks. One of the most beautiful of the starfish, it is one of the few which can be considered a passive filter-feeder.

Spider of the Deep

There are very strange long-legged marine creatures looking like huge spiders; up to two to three feet wide, they abound in both arctic and antarctic waters. In fact recent deep-sea research has shown that sea spiders are very common elements of the abyssal fauna and crawl almost anywhere.

They are very strange creatures indeed. Not true spiders, they are called pycnogonids, and their relationship to the arachnids is unclear. The body of the pycnogonid is reduced about as far as it will go—they are almost all legs. In fact some of the organs that usually are present in the body reside in the first joints of the legs. The eyes (usually four) are gathered together in one mass on a short stalk. The eggs are carried by the male on two legs especially modified for this purpose. The sea spider looks as though it is dribbling two basketballs at once.

Not all the sea spiders are as big as the three-foot *Colossendeis giganteis,* but they all seem to share the same general mode of life. They walk slowly—in the deep sea few things happen fast. They live on the tissues of colonial small animals such as coelenterates and bryozoans. These nutrients are sucked up by the tubular proboscis. The sea spider is like a tall, skinny man, slowly walking around and now and then stopping for a bit of refreshment; an odd way of life for a very improbable form—an experiment of nature that seems to work in the deep sea.

Fear not, starfish. *The sea spider (right) eats the tissues of small colonial animal, such as certain coelenterates and bryozoans. Much as it might wish to, it cannot eat the starfish.*

No body. *Or at least practically none. This 12-legged pycnogonid (below) clearly shows that there isn't much room left in its body for many of its vital organs. They are located in the legs.*

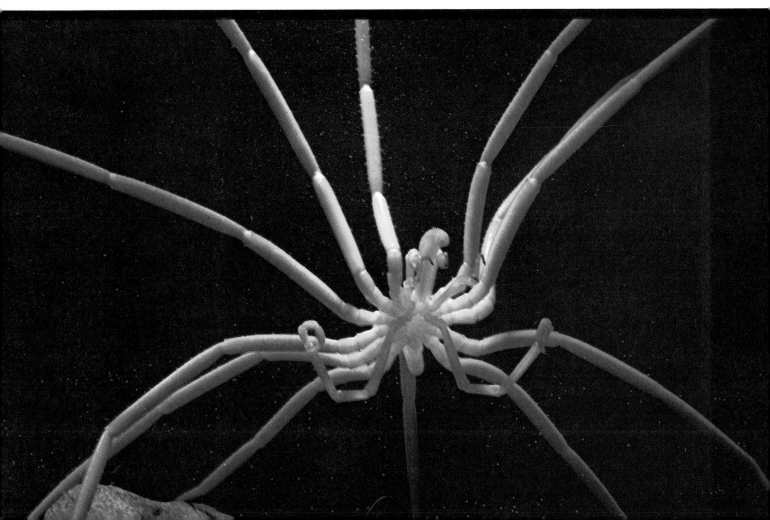

Chapter VI. Living Fossils

Sometimes nature seems to toy with scientists. When we have no information about some events, such as the first appearance of complex fossils at the beginning of the Cambrian period or the mass extinctions of animals at the end of the Mesozoic and Paleozoic eras, we are faced with an almost unbridgable gap in our knowledge. But sometimes, as if by plan, creatures are discovered that fill in the missing spaces in the science of evolution. These creatures are called "living fossils," and they are of two general types. They may be creatures that have survived unchanged from far in the past, or they may be forms that have characteristics indicating they must be related to a "missing link" in an evolutionary sequence.

"Sometimes, as if by plan, creatures are discovered that fill in the missing spaces in the science of evolution."

Since evolution very rarely proceeds on a straight-line basis, we cannot always postulate a "missing link." In man's evolution there were probably several sources for the gene pool that produced *Homo sapiens*. This evolutionary process is termed polyphyletic.

An example: the arthropods were thought to have evolved from the annelid worms. The body tissues of each had similarities: they are both segmented, have heads, and approximately analogous organs. But was there a creature with a wormlike body and legs that might have evolved into the jointed appendages characteristic of the arthropods? In fact, such a creature was found crawling around in tropical woods—it was the onycophoran named *Peripatus,* a creature with a wormlike body and almost-jointed legs.

Peripatus is representative of the transition between arthropods and annelids. In certain Cambrian formations we have also found well-preserved marine onycophorans, which show that *Peripatus* is a living fossil of an ancient group.

One marine creature that has survived practically unchanged for at least 300 million years is the chambered nautilus. It is confined today to certain areas of the South Pacific. Its external shell is one of the most beautiful geometrical structures nature has produced. The nautilus lives in deep water and is at the same time a remote ancestor and a contemporary of the squid, the cuttlefish, and the octopus.

In this chapter we will discuss the living fossils that come from the sea, and we must treat them with reverence since the youngest (the coelacanth) traces its direct lineage back about 400 million years, and the eldest almost 600 million years, longer than any other animal now on earth.

Though a few coelacanths have been caught recently off the Comoro Islands in the Indian Ocean, and many nautiluses have been captured in pots at night in 200 feet of depth, we know practically nothing about their normal habitat or their way of life. There are important lessons to be learned from these creatures, and it is hoped that new ones will be discovered and studied. The sea still holds in store for us scores of such surprises as "living fossils."

Living proof. This unspectacular-looking animal, Neopalina *(top, external view; bottom, internal view), proves the link between the annelid worms and the molluscs to which it belongs. The molluscan traits are obvious, but the annelid characters are shown by its segmentation, visible internally.*

The Patriarch

Walking along a mudflat, one would probably not notice a relatively small bivalved creature, which lives in a burrow and rapidly retracts into it when disturbed. To collect this animal, one must dig down . . . it looks like a clam. Its shell is plain, rather soft, and nondescript; a long muscular structure attached to the downward side of the animal enables it to retract into its burrow. But despite appearances, this animal—*Lingula* (it has no common name)—is not a mollusc. A close examination of its innards reveals a very nonmolluscan arrangement of cavities and organs. *Lingula* also has a lophophore, a device that resembles a coiled arm and contains hairlike structures for filtering particles from the water.

Careful examination of *Lingula*'s shell shows that the two valves are mirror images of each other, like those of the clams; but each of *Lingula*'s valves has a line of symmetry running through itself. Most clams are asymmetric within each valve; they lean to one side or the other. *Lingula* also differs from other brachiopods (the phylum to which it belongs). Most brachiopods have two different shells; the stalk (pedical) is attached to one valve, and the internal coiled structure (lophophore) is attached to the other valve.

But *Lingula*'s importance lies not in its anatomy but in its history. It is the longest-lived animal genus, and a modern *Lingula* is virtually identical to those dating from the Cambrian and perhaps the Precambrian periods. This means *Lingula* is at least 570 million years old!

Lingula is a simple creature; in other words, it is a generalized animal. It has rolled with the punches of the changing nature of the sea, and it has established a life-style that could adapt to almost any event in the earth's dynamic history.

Modern Lingula. *Looking like a clam with a long fleshy tail, this living brachiopod (above) is a member of the oldest and longest-lived modern genus of animals. Although not common, it is found in temperate intertidal waters.*

Ancient story. Lingula *species are commonly found in paleozoic and mesozoic rocks. This slab (below) is of Middle Cambrian age and contains a* Lingula *fossil. The name describes the tongue shape characteristic of the shells. In fossil forms the pedical (stalk) is not preserved.*

Ancient History on a Local Beach

The common horseshoe crab, *Limulus polyphemus,* is a rather fearsome creature at first sight. It is heavily armored and slow-moving, with a long, pointed tail and spikes projecting from its jointed shell. Like *Lingula, Limulus* has been around since the Cambrian period. Changes that it has undergone in response to the dynamic oceans have been sufficiently great to convince scientists that the present genus is not the same as the Cambrian form. But the similarities are striking.

Limulus feeds on marine worms, which it churns up as it burrows through the mud. Oddly enough, it is a fine swimmer, but it flips over on its back to do so and then uses its tail-spike, or telson, to right itself. Despite a bizarre appearance, it is a gentle creature; it cannot bite and the small pincers on its appendages are only for feeding and walking.

Many an aspiring paleontologist has done a double take on observing the larvae of *Limulus* for the first time. Superficially these larvae are dead ringers for those of trilobites. One of the most intriguing questions in paleontology is whether or not trilobites are indeed related to horseshoe crabs. The general evidence suggests that they are not related, because the horseshoe crabs of the Cambrian were well established when the earliest trilobites appeared.

The horseshoe crab is not a true crab but is a member of the group called Xiphosurans. Another member of this group is the now-extinct sea scorpion, which flourished in the Silurian period. These sea scorpions, which were not true scorpions but Eurypterids, grew up to 12 feet long and were probably fierce predators. They may have forced the newly evolving fish of the early Paleozoic to grow the kinds of armor exhibited by most early ostracoderms and placoderms.

The Eurypterids are gone, leaving *Limulus* to stalk our nearshore regions alone—a living fossil in slow, gentle triumph.

Not too archaic to mate. *Horeshoe crabs are common residents of modern beaches, as they were on ancient ones. This pair (below) are in the act of mating to insure the future of the lineage.*

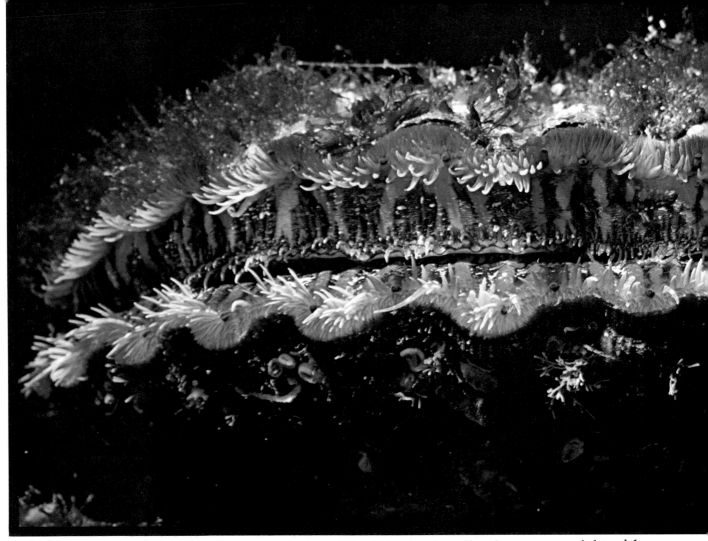

To See Better

The human eye, and the vertebrate eye in general, is a wonder. Photographers must use a wide variety of lenses and tricks to approach the sharpness and depth of focus that we normally get in our everyday vision. Our stereovision is almost unmatched, except among the birds and the great apes.

Man does not hold the patent on successfully evolved eyes. The vision of hawks is legendary. The average arthropod may have dozens or even hundreds of eyes—individual lenses that make up the compound eye. And among the vertebrates, there are the three eyes of the lamprey (the third eye is formed from the pineal organ). The molluscs, which continuously surprise the casual observer with their complexity, have produced a number of different eyes among their ranks.

The blue-eyed scallop is a strange sight with rows of beautiful eyespots lining the edge of its mantle. Among the molluscs is the squid, an invertebrate with the best eyes in the sea. The two eyes are enormous, efficient, and sometimes of different sizes. Some researchers think the size difference allows one eye to function better in the low-light condition of deep water and the other to work efficiently in the upper photic zone. The comparison of the squid eye with that of man has long fascinated biologists. The squid eye has almost the same structure as the human eye. But in the squid the lens is moved forward and back to focus, while in man the lens is stretched by muscles. And the squid's photoreceptors are pointed at the source of light instead of away from it as are man's.

Nature also displayed acumen when it composed the eye of our venerable friend *Limu-*

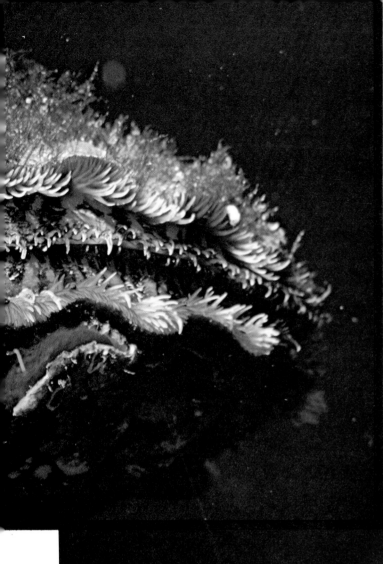

lus. At a recent conference in Europe, a fascinating paper was presented about the shape of each element of the compound eye of the horseshoe crab (the individual structure is called an ommatidium). Each light receptor is the exact shape that physicists calculated as the perfect light receptor! This shape is a complicated parabolic configuration, which gives the animal a series of highly efficient light-gathering lenses.

The study of similarities in structures is called comparative anatomy, and researchers in this field have yet to determine how three different phyla of animals—arthropods, molluscs, and chordates—produced three different but equally efficient eyes.

Pretty blue eyes. *Rows of functional eyes line the mantle of the common scallop (left).*

Compound eye. *Each element of the horseshoe crab's eye (below) is a mathematically perfect light receptor, based on a complicated formula.*

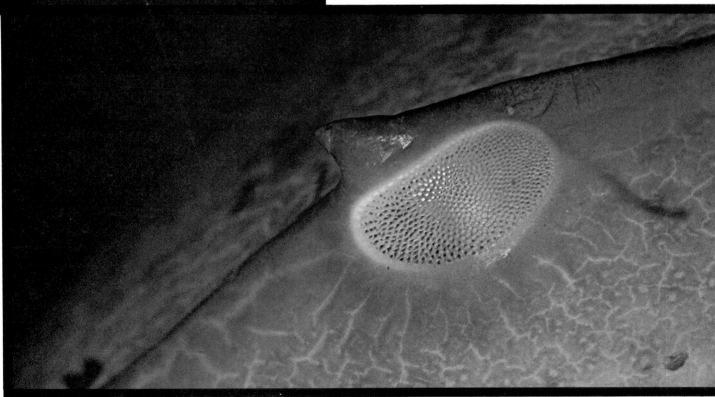

Chapter VII. In The Beginning

There have been many theories on the origin of our planet. Ever since man appeared, the origin of the world around him has been an unending source of wonder and conjecture. By chance, or by some wise intuition, most of the legends of the creation of the earth and of life begin in the sea.

According to the Chinese legend of creation, "at first there was nothing. Time passed and something split in two: the two were male

---

"Most legends of the creation of life begin in the sea."

---

and female. These two produced two more, and these two produced P'an Ku, the first being, the great Man, the Creator."

The Egyptians call the moment of creation "The First Time." The most ancient Egyptian account begins with the Waters of Chaos, Nun, the primeval ocean, and the god who created himself—the Sun God—whose name was Atum meaning everything and nothing. Later, when he began to rule creation his name became Ra. Thus, Atum—or Atum-Ra, the Sun God—arose uncreated from the Waters of Chaos and *became*.

In the Greek myth first came Chaos and before that nothing. But man's mind cannot think nothing, so Chaos contained the seeds of all things that "were to be." And Earth, while she slept, gave birth to Uranus, the sky. He showered his mother with rain so that trees shot up, flowers bloomed, grass grew, and animals and birds were born in the forests and grasslands. Lakes filled up and rivers flowed down to the seas.

In the Rig-Veda of Indian mythology, one of the creation stories begins with the rolling primeval waters, in which evolved a golden egg. And from this egg came the lord of all being who made heaven and earth and bestowed life and breath on the creatures. Prajapati, lord and father of creatures, was the title given to this life-giving deity.

The ancient Mexican legend of the Mixtec Indian begins with these words: "In the year and in the day of obscurity and darkness, where there were as yet no year and no day, the world was chaos sunk in darkness." The whole earth was covered with water. Green slime floated on the surface of the water and the scum moved gently in the dark. One day came the god, in human form, and his beautiful goddess. They raised a steep cliff over the abyss of water and on top of it built a fine dwelling for themselves. On the topmost point of the cliff, they laid a copper ax, edge up, and on this sharp edge rested the sky.

We all know the biblical version in which "God created the heaven and the earth. And the earth was without form and void; and the Spirit of God moved upon the face of the waters." Actually the Bible provides some generally sound guidelines for the genesis of the earth and life, but the time periods involved must be changed from days to millions of years. Aside from the minor details of sequence, there was first the earth, then water; at the same time as water there was air, then life, and man. But there is still life evolving, and man is not the endpoint or perfection of evolution, but an important point in space and time.

Rebirth. With every eruption of a volcano, new rock is being added to the earth's crust, new water to the atmosphere and oceans. This was the ancient source of much of the early land surfaces, the primeval ocean, the primitive atmosphere.

67

Rock luau. *The new surfaces of cooling lava are of two types. The names were given by Hawaiians, who see many lava flows: Pahoehoe (above) is ropy and folded; Aa is rough and vesicular.*

Setting the Stage ...

Today there are two explanations of the beginning of our world—the catastrophe theory and the condensation theory; the latter is now more widely accepted. Both theories agree, however, that the action started about 4.6 billion years ago. The catastrophe theory suggests that the earth and other planets were torn out of the sun by a giant star.

The condensation theory proposes that the sun was formed from a large cloud of dust and gas that began to concentrate in the universe. As the sun increased in size, its gravitational force grew, and more and more cosmic dust and gases were attracted to it. The planets then began to form out of the original dust cloud.

For some 500 million years, the core of the earth was solid; it was a comparatively cool mass of iron and silicates, its temperature being less than 2000° C. Some of the elements the earth had pulled into itself, like uranium, thorium, and potassium, were radioactive, and their decay gradually heated the earth until its internal temperature rose to about 7000° C. The iron in the earth was one of the first elements to melt. Since it was heavier than most other elements, it sank to the center, forcing the lighter rocks that were in its path to the surface. This accounts for the molten ironlike core that exists today. The layer that formed above the core is called the mantle; it is a churning plastic mass of heavy silicate minerals. The shifting of this material, spurred by the heat rising from the core, generates the energy powering the movement of the uppermost layer—the crust. This crustal movement is popularly called continental drift. The enormous interior heat, producing convective currents within the earth, also carried rocks and gases to the surface. These rocks and gases finally became more or less stabilized and after millions of years formed the first land, ocean, and atmosphere. There were first only desolate expanses of rocky surface; the earth was dotted by scattered bodies of water. Lightning and solar flares were displayed without the interference of an oxygen and ozone shield. The whole face of the earth was a vast landscape of flame-throwing volcanoes spewing out lava and hot geysers leaping into the unbreathable air. It was millions of years before this burning caldron cooled enough to form a thin crust of solid rocks covering the earth. All this probably happened under skies loaded with heavy clouds from which the rain fell and slowly eroded the naked rocks. Oceans formed. The nest of life was being readied for its inhabitants.

Fireworks. Lavas from volcano craters and vents (below) are rich in iron and magnesium minerals. When they cool quickly, as usually happens, they form the rock basalt.

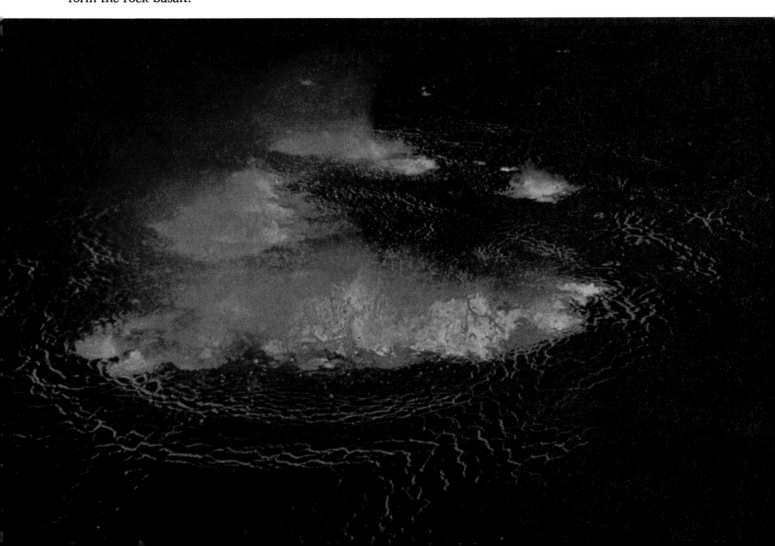

Birth of the Sea

When the ancient Chinese poet wrote that Creation was something that came from nothing, he touched on the truth. Who could have dared dream that a loose cloud of stardust and gases could have ultimately produced our earth with its oceans, land, atmosphere, and life? That the whole process took approximately 4.5 billion years does not diminish the wonder of its happening.

The most elementary form of life needs water. But where did water come from? When our earth formed, its gravitational field was not strong enough to hold an atmosphere, and most of the lighter gases, like hydrogen and water vapor, escaped into space. When the planet solidified about 4.5 billion years ago, gases were trapped in the cooling rocks. Subsequent volcanic eruptions and lava flows released large quantities of gases including nitrogen, ammonia, methane, water vapor, and carbon monoxide plus carbon dioxide. The water vapor was decomposed by ultraviolet radiation into its components—oxygen and hydrogen. The hydrogen was lost to space, and the oxygen probably reacted with carbon monoxide to form carbon dioxide. This kind of atmosphere was said to be "reducing," or "oxygen hungry." As the earth cooled further, however, water vapor began to condense into rain, which helped form the early seas. The release of liquid water from the earth's interior also contributed to the growing oceans.

Oxygen was not a major constituent of the atmosphere until photosynthesis evolved. Plant cells removed carbon dioxide from the atmosphere and liberated oxygen. Eventually, oxygen was produced faster than it could be reduced, or consumed, by hydrogen or carbon dioxide, and the atmosphere as we know it today began to form.

Meanwhile, the oceans were still growing, being supplied with water from volcanoes, geysers, and lava flows. Such "juvenile" waters are still feeding our oceans today, but to a very small extent.

The atmosphere surrounding the earth extends several hundred miles above the surface. It is 78 percent nitrogen and 21 percent oxygen with the remaining one percent largely inert gases and water vapor. Water covers about 70 percent of the earth's surface, most of it in the oceans which have an average depth of 12,450 feet. The three layers of the biosphere—the ocean, the land surface, and the atmosphere—actually make up only a fraction of the earth's mass. It is in this fragile, thin envelope that life began about 3.2 billion years ago.

And the rains came. The rains on the earliest earth came from waters in the atmosphere liberated from the rock of the mantle. Most igneous rock (rock crystallized from molten magma) contains some water in its makeup, and this juvenile water was released on the primitive earth, as it is today, through geysers (above and right) and volcanoes.

The Shields for the Earth

Although the sun's light provides the basic energy of life, unshielded ultraviolet radiation is deadly to living tissue. The skies present other dangers to cells in the form of cosmic rays; these rays have very short wavelengths and travel at incredible speed. They can penetrate all but the thickest shield and wreak havoc with the genetic and chemical substances of life.

It was not until ozone was produced in the atmosphere that life on land and in the surface layers of the water was possible.

Ordinary oxygen gas is composed of two atoms of oxygen securely combined. Ozone has a third oxygen atom loosely hanging on to these two and this atom makes ozone a chemically active gas. Some oxygen in the atmosphere is converted to ozone by lightning, but ultraviolet rays from the sun are the major force turning oxygen into ozone. In time this conversion of oxygen into ozone formed a concentrated layer of ozone 15 miles above the earth. This layer was a shield which prevented ultraviolet rays from damaging plant and animal cells and gave life as we know it a chance to survive.

some equipment he designed for an American satellite reported intense radiation at the equatorial region beginning about 600 miles above the earth's surface. Van Allen made further investigations and reported to the scientific community on this vital shield that protects us.

Our knowledge of the effects of cosmic and ultraviolet radiation has led to some strange speculations in the recent scientific literature. The earth's magnetic poles are known to have reversed at several points in time. If these reversals were not instantaneous, as many specialists believe, it is likely that the Van Allen belt was dissipated due to the lack of a magnetic field. Is it possible that some of the times of mass extinction among animal and plant groups resulted from this?

Or consider that even today, with all our shields, we are still bombarded by cosmic rays—not enough to interfere with our daily lives and physical development, but perhaps enough to show up over the whole span of a person's life. Is it possible that senility really is the result of brain cells (which the body cannot regenerate) slowly dying from the lifetime cosmic ray bombardment?

Astronauts in earth orbit, while outside the ozone shield, are still protected by the Van Allen belt and of course by their space ships, but those on the moon receive full exposure. It is clear that past lunar explorers were not grossly affected, but it is still to early to know if long-term complications will arise. Future lunar colonists must be able to shield themselves from cosmic rays or the colonies will be very short-lived.

A huge region, like a great inflated automobile tube, surrounds our earth some 60,000 miles in space. It is composed of charged atomic particles—protons and neutrons—that are believed to have streamed out from the sun's surface during solar disturbances. At a certain point, these particles interacted with the earth's magnetic field which trapped them. This recently discovered region is called the Van Allen belt, and like the ozone layer it acts as a shield to prevent too much radiation from falling on our planet. The American physicist James Van Allen discovered this natural phenomenon when

A view from space. This satellite photograph (left) shows the cloud cover over the Western Hemisphere, but not the invisible ozone shield or the Van Allen belt. These protective shields lie above the level at which the satellite orbits.

Chapter VIII. Origin of Life

Every branch of science has its own definition of life. Biologically, the basic form of life is the cell—though new biology theories suggest that the connections *between* cells are also part of the living substance.

Chemically, carbon is the element without which life as we know it could not exist.

According to physics, the common denominators of both living and nonliving substances are protons, neutrons, and electrons.

"The difficulties of defining life are simple compared to the problems of tracing its origins and evolution."

"Life," says scientist J. D. Bernal, "is the embodiment within a certain volume of a self-maintaining chemical process."

And Sir Julian Huxley believed that "No single link can be said to be *living;* no hard and fast line can be drawn between the living and nonliving. Life, from the viewpoint of the scientific observer is a self-regulating, self-repairing physiochemical complex mechanism."

In any event life came into existence, and no one has yet been able to define precisely its countless functions and its varied manifestations. The difficulties of defining life are simple compared to the problems of tracing its origins and evolution. Many conditions had to be present before even the first faint evidences of life could appear. First, the earth had to have a sun that was hot enough and had a life-span long enough for living organisms to evolve. Since it seems to have taken about one billion years for life to evolve, only special stars qualified. A planet's distance from a star is also critical, since too much or too little energy from its sun would make it impossible for any organism to develop. The size of a planet is also important, since the planet's mass affects its gravitational force. Our earth was able to allow life to evolve because, among other things, the earth's gravity was strong enough to hold oxygen and water in the atmosphere, yet weak enough to allow hydrogen to escape, making the atmosphere suitable for organic evolution. Temperature is another crucial factor. In space it fluctuates from hundreds of degrees below zero to the heat of stars whose interior temperature can reach one billion degrees C. Life as we know it can exist only within a very narrow temperature range. Measured on a thermometer 100 km. long, a section only 0.1 cm. long allows for the existence of life.

Every living organism seems to require about 20 chemical elements and traces of several others to maintain life. At least 95 percent of all protoplasm is made up of hydrogen, carbon, nitrogen, oxygen, phosphorus, and sulphur, plus small quantities of potassium, sodium, magnesium and calcium and traces of other metals and compounds. Life without water would have been impossible, and it seems that all the essentials for life are universally present in seawater. As the most important component of protoplasm, water accounts for approximately 80 to 90 percent of all living matter. And because water is a universal solvent, it could carry all elements necessary for nurturing life, in suspension or solution, and take them from areas where they were abundant to other areas in the ocean where they were scarce. This gave life a better chance to start on our planet.

Ultraviolet light, if it reached the earth unshielded today, would kill most organisms.

Four billion years ago, however, ultraviolet energy established the groundwork for life to begin. These powerful rays split the inorganic molecules that were in the primitive atmosphere. Some of these fragments reunited to form organic compounds such as aldehydes and amino acids. Since these organic particles were heavier than most atmospheric material, they sank through the atmosphere to the surface of the ocean; they also fell on land and were washed into the sea by rain. Inorganic particles were also washed down from land as a result of rock weathering. For millions of years these compounds were collected in the oceans, and under the stimulus of heat and ultraviolet rays many of them joined together to form bigger and more complicated substances, thus making the ocean rich in a wide variety of organic molecules. The basic substances of life were now present.

Simple beginnings. Every organism shares things with every other one: the need for food and for room and the need to reproduce. All life is composed of a few chemicals, and it all began in the sea.

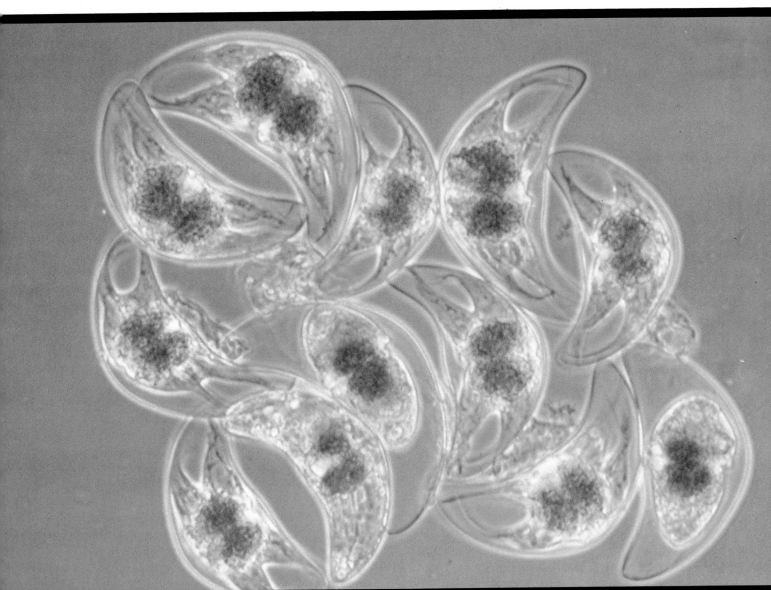

Energy of Life

The energy for all the living things on earth comes from the sun. And the energy of the sun comes from the atom. In 1905 Albert Einstein formulated his famous equation, $E = mc^2$—the energy locked into a mass is equal to the mass multiplied by the square of the speed of light. This discovery changed our entire view of the universe. Einstein's theory led to our understanding that our sun is basically a fusion reactor like the hydrogen bomb. In other words, continuous nuclear reaction keeps the sun working.

This energy from the sun gave the impetus to nonliving substances to bind, grow, change, divide, and eventually live. The sun's energy provided warmth to stir the chemical broth and to prod interactions. The earth itself, hot, seething, and unstable, released its gases and water vapor which churned in the atmosphere. Great storms raged and caused electrical disturbances. Lightning then became another source of energy, combining stable atmospheric nitrogen with oxygen and converting it into nitrate. But the major source of these nitrogen-oxygen compounds is biological systems. They can only be synthesized by nitrogen-fixing bacteria and without these living nitrogen fixers and the limited help from lightning the most essential element of a protein—nitrogen—would be unavailable for plants and animals.

The sun is still essential for life's continuance. Without the sun's warmth earth would be uninhabitable and without light energy and utilization of it by plants the earth would be uninhabited.

Energy. Lightning is raw power—a source of the first life energy. The electricity actually flows from the ground upward, not downward as it appears to go. Even the energy for lightning ultimately traces back to the sun, which drives the atmosphere.

77

Beginnings

Organic chemicals occurring in the sea had to be presented to each other in the right concentration in order to react. This situation is similar to the ignition of an explosive in air—when the concentration of explosive is too high, it just burns; when the concentration is too low, nothing happens.

The organic chemicals in the early sea were in low concentrations, and there had to be some mechanism to get them together for life to form. Fortunately, two natural phenomena, which can be observed in the modern laboratory, were working then.

Certain clay minerals have the unusual property of adsorption—that is, they collect and accumulate substances on their surfaces. This natural phenomenon leads to the second. When oily or fatty substances collect on the right medium, poorly understood ionic forces induce the resulting globs to behave in a rather lifelike manner. These accumulations of organic molecules are called coacervate drops, and they are thought to be an early stage in organic evolution.

Coacervates are fascinating laboratory toys. They grow by accreting new molecules from the watery environment, and when they reach a certain size, they divide. They almost seem to move of their own accord. But they are not living—or are they?

The coacervate drops in the primeval sea broth were probably made up of prototype enzymes and complex carbon (organic) compounds. They contained the basic substances of life. Enzymes are essential to all living things, and they control the chemical reactions taking place within a cell. They are basically proteins to which a nonprotein substance, such as a vitamin, can attach. As catalysts, they change the rate of chemical reactions without being changed perma-

nently themselves. An enzyme may separate a molecule, or it may bring molecules together by uniting, temporarily, with a specific part of a molecule. After the appropriate chemical reaction has occurred, the unchanged enzyme breaks away, leaving a newly synthesized chemical compound.

In the organic evolutionary process, enzyme development may be second in importance

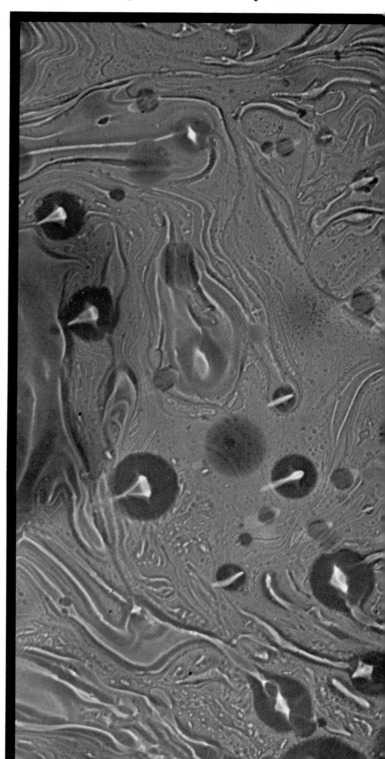

only to the accumulation of chemicals into those coacervatelike droplets.

A subsequent event vital in the origin of life was the appearance of nucleic acids (DNA and RNA). These chemicals had the ability to reproduce themselves. ATP (adenosine triphosphate), the compound that spreads and stores energy in the cell, was also present. These are the essences of life.

The ingredients for life now pervaded millions of watery places over the primitive earth. Life was finally ready to begin. Or had it already begun?

Drops of life. *Under the microscope's eye, drops of some oily substances in water form almost lifelike coacervates. The observer must continually remind himself that they are behaving the way they do because of ionic forces.*

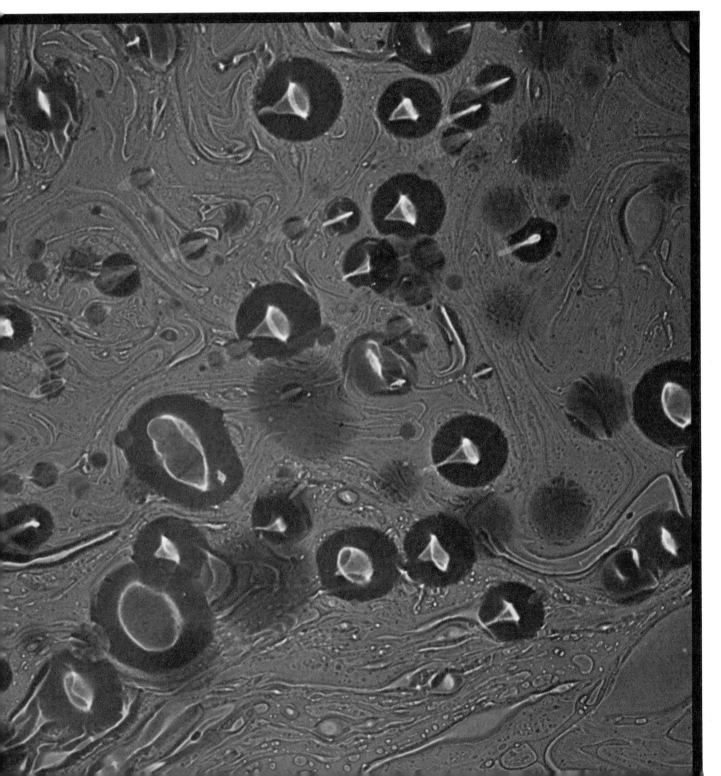

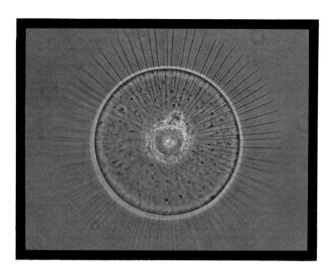

The Cell

After millions of years of chemical evolution, the primordial sea soup yielded a living creature—a one-celled entity that could reproduce, take in food, and grow. In 3.5 billion years, evolution has progressed from single-celled animals to man, a conglomeration of billions upon billions of cells.

It was not until 1663 that an Englishman named Robert Hooke, while looking at slices of cork under his primitive microscope, noticed it was composed of little individual units that reminded him of the honeycomb pattern of a beehive. He called these minute compartments "cells." One hundred and seventy-five years later, in the early part of the nineteenth century, the groundwork of modern cell theory was established; in 1838, the German botanist Matthias Schleiden pointed out that the cell was the structural unit of all vegetable matter. One year later, another German scientist, Theodor Schwann, made the startling realization that "cells are organisms and entire animals and plants are aggregates of these organisms arranged according to definite laws."

A cell can be a self-sufficient organism, like an amoeba, that actively moves about and hunts food, or it can be part of a more highly organized creature, closely integrated with

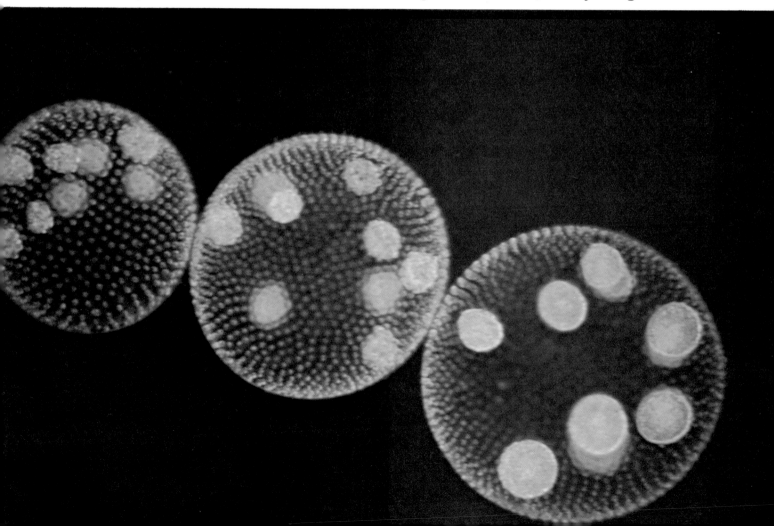

other cells to perform more specific functions. Cells come in a wide variety of shapes and sizes. They can appear as rods, spheres, spirals, boxes, saucers, or just plain blobs and can vary in size from the yolk of an egg, which is the size of a golfball, to a bacteria three or four millionths of a meter long. They can be supported by silica, carbonate, cellulose, hard proteins, or a membrane.

Internally, cells show a high degree of organization and complexity. Every cell has an outer wall or membrane that encloses a bit of cytoplasm—a semiliquid substance in which the life activities of the cell are carried out. Within the cytoplasm is a nucleus, the control center of cell functions and the place where hereditary material is stored. Also within the cytoplasm are a host of other structures, each with a specific job and each contributing to the cell's well-being.

The cell is the basic unit of life, but what is life? We usually consider a living entity something that can take in nutrients, can grow, is sensitive to its evironment, and can reproduce. Can there be life without any of these criteria? Viruses do not take in food, but rather control the life processes of another cell and make it work for them. Are viruses alive? Mineral crystals can increase in size and take in additional materials as they do so. Are they alive? When does a nonliving inanimate object become a living, animate one? What mysterious force or vital spark turned nonliving into living? This question has been pondered by many great minds through the ages. Perhaps it is one question that will never really be answered.

The functions of cells. Each single-celled diatom (upper left and below) is a self-contained unit that carries on its life functions perfectly. Certain cells form aggregates of individuals, and some functions, such as reproduction in Volvox (lower left), are carried out by the colony. Still other cells are part of a complex organism, like fish and man.

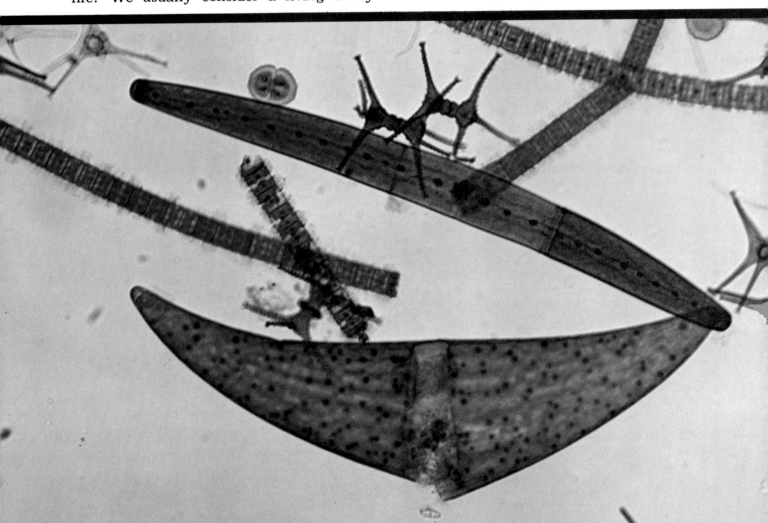

The Algae Mat

Possibly the oldest evidences of life are to be found in stromatolites—large, dome-shaped layers of mud particles, which were trapped in mats of algae. In Precambrian times these sediments slowly developed their characteristic form in tidal waters. Today they are found all over the world, sometimes on mountaintops miles from the sea. The stromatolites and their encasements have helped retain some of the organic compounds formed 2.5 billion years ago.

Most of the fossil algae has completely disappeared, but algae filaments (threads) have been discovered in cherts (pieces of flintlike quartz) scattered through limestones. Most extraordinary stromatolites have been discovered near Helena, Montana; they are as much as 15 feet thick, extending for thousands of feet along the vein from the bottom to the top of the Helena Dolomite. The cross-section of these stromatolites looks like heads of cabbage vertically sliced. Rod-shaped bacteria, filaments of blue green algae, and possibly fungi have been preserved in cherts. These fossil remains also contain traces of eight amino acids and include the oldest known multicellular fossils—dating back about 1.9 billion years.

More recently, rod- and coccus-shaped bacteria have been found in organic, rich black cherts of the Fig Tree series in South Africa. They are more than 3 billion years old, and are the oldest known fossils.

Even today stromatolites are being assembled by blue green algae, which still extract lime from the surrounding water. Such stromatolitic formations are found around Australia, Bermuda, and the Bahama Islands.

Floating for four billion years. This algal layer, afloat in the seas off the Great Barrier Reef, may be an exact duplicate of its ancient counterpart.

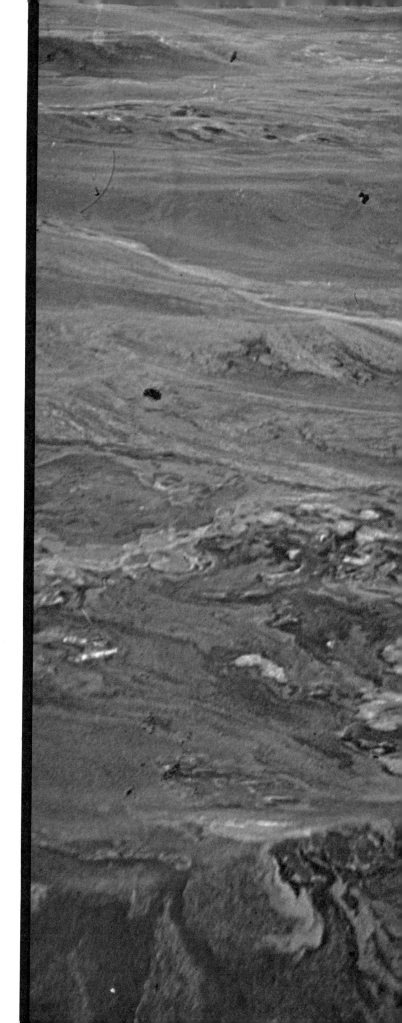

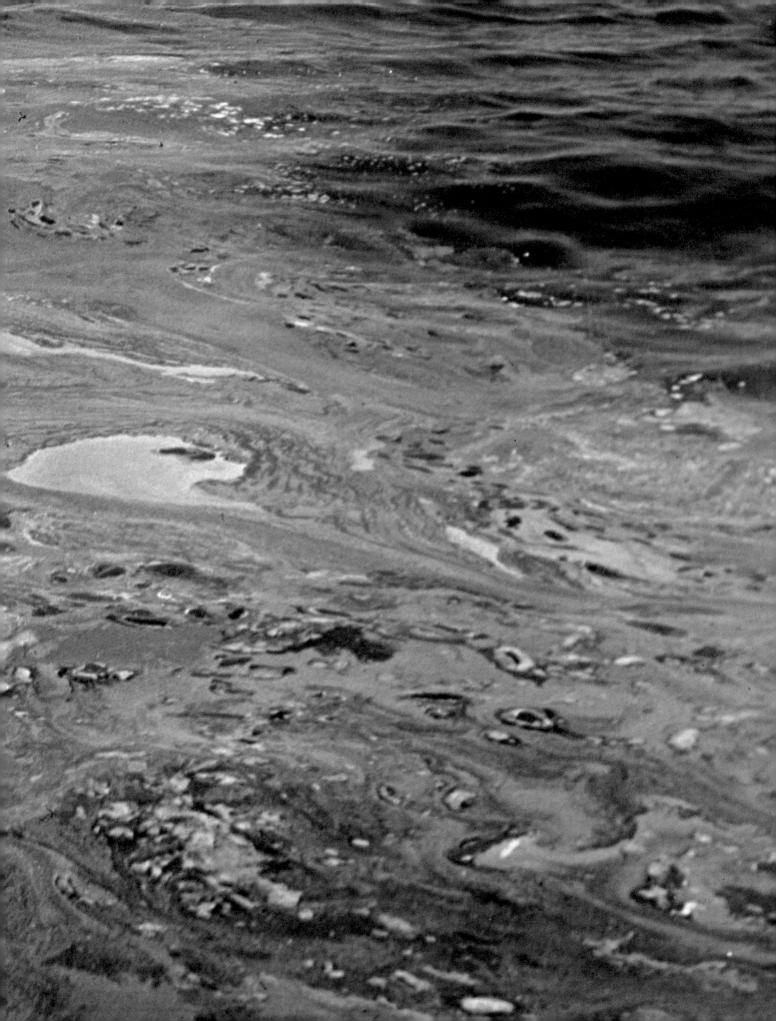

The Nucleus of Progress

The cell is the building block of all life-forms —from unicellular plants and animals to man. At one time scientists believed all cells were similar in structure—each having a cell wall or membrane, a nucleus, and various other minute structures scattered throughout the cytoplasm. However, within the past quarter century the perfection of the electron microscope has revolutionized knowledge about the way cells are organized. It is now understood that not one, but two different kinds of cells exist among living organisms: the eucaryotic cell, which has a nucleus and is characteristic of plants, animals, protozoa, and most groups of algae, and the procaryotic cell, which does not have a nucleus and is the unit of structure in bacteria and blue green algae.

Bacteria and blue green algae are perhaps the oldest living forms of life on earth. This has led some scientists to suggest that the procaryotic cell type is more primitive and probably lead to the eucaryotic cell plan. In both cell types there is a membrane envelope that surrounds the cytoplasm. The nucleus of the eucaryotic cell is also membrane bound. The nuclear material of the procaryotic is free within the cytoplasm. The genetic material in the eucaryotic nucleus is in the form of structural units called chromosomes. Every cell in our bodies has 46 chromosomes except sperm or egg cells which possess half this number. However, information about procaryotic cells indicates the genetic material is in only one long chromosome.

Eucaryotic cells contain other membrane-bound structures like mitochondria, organelles concerned with cellular respiration;

Life without a nucleus. *The blue green algae (below) are about the simplest form of life known, but probably also the most successful.*

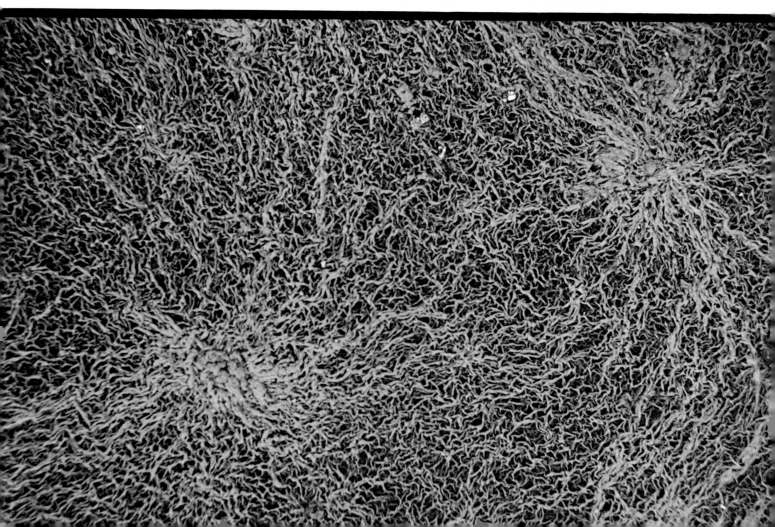

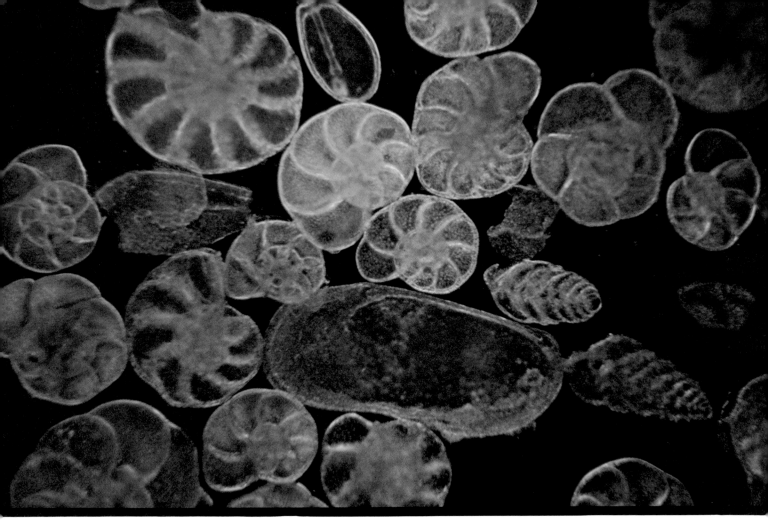

lysosomes, small packages that hold enzymes; and vacuoles, liquid-filled bodies that hold cellular products. In procaryotic cells, there are no such membrane-bound compartments; the only major internal regions are the unbound nucleus and cytoplasm. The machinery for respiration and/or photosynthesis is located in the cytoplasmic membrane that bounds the cell. Metabolic enzymes are located in the cytoplasm.

Most free-living microorganisms inhabit a hypotonic environment (that is, an environment in which the concentration of water is higher outside the cell than within it). Therefore water will enter the cell in an effort to balance the concentrations. If this phenomenon is not checked, the cell will swell and eventually burst open. Eucaryotic cells have met this challenge by using contractile vacuoles, specialized vacuoles that work like pumps to eliminate water. Pro-

Shelled cells. Foraminifera (above) are protozoans that have developed shells, some of which form much of the deep-ocean oozes.

caryotic cells lack vacuoles and maintain water balance by having a rigid cell wall that inhibits water from moving in. This limits procaryotic cells in their movement and ability to secure food. They cannot flow like an amoeba or swim like a paramecium.

From the evolutionary point of view, scientists ponder whether eucaryotes arose from procaryotes or if the two types arose independently billions of years ago. Some evidence suggests that the cellular organelles found in eucaryotes were once free-living entities that took up an existence in primitive procaryotic cells. If such was the course of evolution, this was a monumental step forward, since all higher forms of life are made up of eucaryotic cells.

85

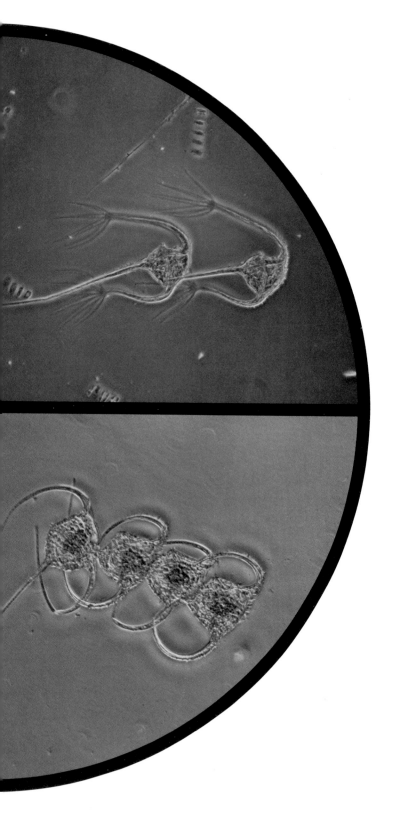

The First Foods

Evolution does not work in a straight line, always producing better and more efficient forms of life. Actually evolution does not have any intent or direction at all, and it is only by chance that certain life forms develop and survive. Many experiments fail. So it was with the primitive heterotrophs, which depended upon organic matter as a source of food. Many of them surely were altered through those first few billion years with various chemical systems being developed and failing.

But some of these heterotrophs slowly began to evolve into autotrophs—organisms that could put together all or some of the organic nutrients they needed from inorganic substances. Modern autotrophs have evolved into forms that can assimilate a whole range of nutrients, including substances that are far from the common notion of food. Among the bacteria, especially, are species that specialize in living off various chemicals. These chem-autotrophs include *Beggiatoa alba*, which utilizes sulfur for its nutrient needs. Still other cells developed a way to use light from the sun to supply them with the energy to convert inorganic material to organic substances. These cells, called photoautotrophs, all developed a system of light-sensitive pigments with which they could capture solar energy and use it to make food. The process they utilized—photosynthesis, basically the conversion of light energy to chemical energy—was perhaps the most important and crucial step in the continuing evolution of life.

Food from air and water. Photosynthetic cells like these dinoflagellates (right and left) create their own food—and food for most of the living world by the complex process of photosynthesis. As yet man has been unable to duplicate this process.

Photosynthesis is the conversion of two stable molecules—water, H_2O, and carbon dioxide, CO_2—into a more complicated organic molecule—a sugar ($C_6H_{12}O_6$)—and oxygen (O_2). This reaction is stated simply in the following formula:

$$6\,CO_2 + 6\,H_2O \text{ light } \quad C_6H_{12}O_6 + 6\,O_2$$

Plants utilize light energy to produce the energy-rich compounds ATP and NADPH. These substances contain high-energy bonds, which are the result of a complicated conversion of light energy into chemical energy. They supply the power to change CO_2 to a simple sugarlike glucose. Through polymerization, a step-by-step assemblage of simple compounds into more complex ones, plants can convert simple sugars into needed substances like starches and cellulose.

Photosynthesis not only created a new supply of organic nutrients for all heterotrophic organisms, ultimately including man, but also liberated free oxygen into the atmosphere. This apparently trivial by-product of photosynthesis, the release of oxygen, changed the evolution of the world and its inhabitants. It not only provided the planet with a protective ozone layer but also led to the evolution of a whole new line of organisms. These creatures had oxidative metabolism; that is, they could utilize oxygen in their energy-producing processes. These organisms had somehow hit upon the food-to-energy conversion system which has become a model for all higher forms of life. It allows a more efficient transformation of food into the free energy needed by the cell to do its mechanical, chemical, and biological work.

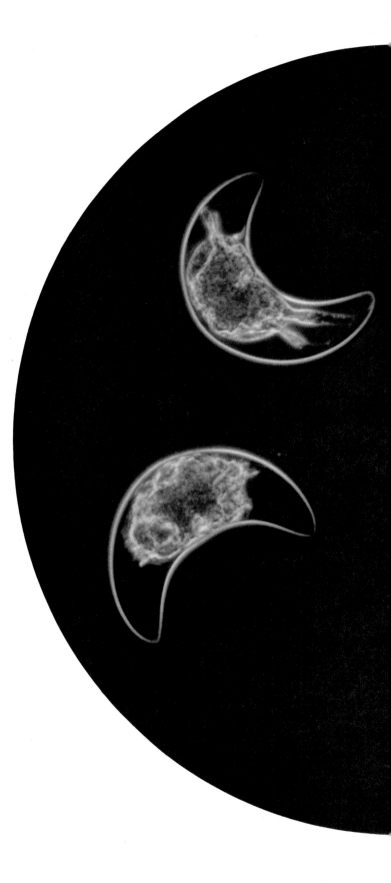

Stay High. These dinoflagellates are motile enabling them to seed the sunlit surface waters (right and left). The delicate extensions of their body may serve to retard their sinking by increasing the total surface area affected by friction.

Chapter IX. The Invertebrate Experiment

In our 4.5 billion-year-old detective story concerning the origin of the world and life on it, we have been left with an incredible number of special clues—fossils, or remains of living organisms preserved in various ways for up to billions of years. Paleontologists (students of ancient life-forms and their habitats) patiently try to put together the history of the earth from fossils since they offer the most convincing evidence of the process of evolution.

Natural catastrophes have always caused untold damage and mass death. To the paleontologist, these catastrophes are major sources of information regarding the disappearance of species or changes in their forms.

"Fossils offer the most convincing evidence of the process of evolution."

In one catastrophe several thousand years ago, a wooly mammoth was frozen in the Siberian ice. Its death was so sudden that the food in its stomach was preserved intact and the flesh of the animal was found to be edible. Fossils, however, are not usually so helpfully intact. The detectives of our past have to study innumerable clues and follow up small hints, probing through miles of rocks searching for their bits and pieces of evidence. Their tools are usually nothing more dramatic than a pick or a spade, a pocket knife, and various brushes. For the most part, too, paleontologists have to count on more ordinary methods of preservation; these only give them a one out of ten chance to find some fossils that will give even a very limited picture of any period of life.

Since only a few groups of animals and plants have skeletons capable of being preserved as fossils, one authority has estimated that of the 3000 species of plants and animals in a modern reef community, only 50 to 75 are recognizable after death. We cannot, therefore, depend on the fossil record as a sample of all past life. But since invertebrates were evolution's first experiment with living forms, any traces they left in fossil forms are most important clues.

Quick burial is the simplest and most dependable form of fossilization. The "reinforcing" process during which a shell or a bone becomes coated and its pores or canals filled by a solution of calcium carbonate also provides fine fossils. Petrification, one of the most common types of preservation, takes place when part of the shell is replaced by a mineral in solution. An animal's form is preserved when groundwater dissolves an organism's shell but leaves the shell's impression on the enclosing substance. Still another method of fossilization occurs when the proteins in the dead organism break down by oxidation or bacterial action. Carbon, the only stable element in organic tissues, remains as a black film, and the process is called carbonization. Today tracks, trails, burrows, teeth marks, and excretions of organisms provide evidence of former living things, even when they leave neither impressions nor parts of their actual organisms. Fossils also help date rocks. By knowing the age of one species we can infer the ages of others depending upon whether they lie above or below the known species.

The continuous thread. *Empty shells on a beach (above) may become fossils as the beach sediments become rock and the shells are buried within. The fossils (below) are from the Miocene period, but they were once just shells on the beach.*

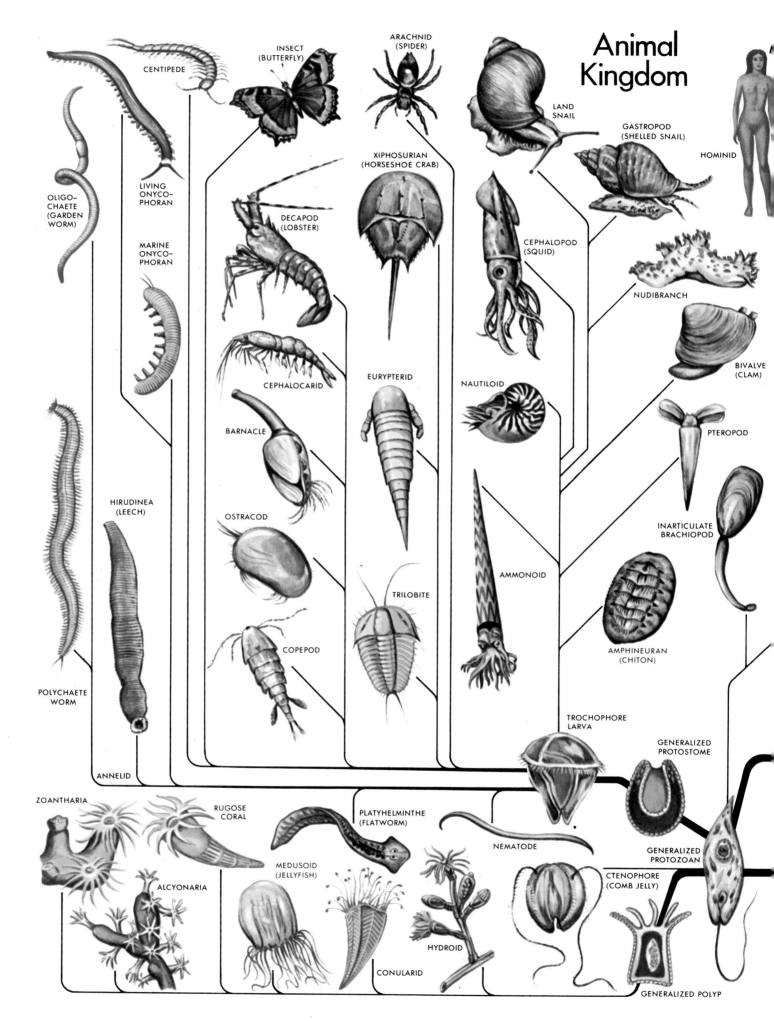

Animal Kingdom

CENTIPEDE

INSECT
(BUTTERFLY)

ARACHNID
(SPIDER)

LAND
SNAIL

GASTROPOD
(SHELLED SNAIL)

HOMINID

LIVING
ONYCO-
PHORAN

OLIGO-
CHAETE
(GARDEN
WORM)

MARINE
ONYCO-
PHORAN

DECAPOD
(LOBSTER)

XIPHOSURIAN
(HORSESHOE CRAB)

CEPHALOPOD
(SQUID)

NUDIBRANCH

CEPHALOCARID

EURYPTERID

NAUTILOID

BIVALVE
(CLAM)

BARNACLE

PTEROPOD

HIRUDINEA
(LEECH)

OSTRACOD

INARTICULATE
BRACHIOPOD

AMMONOID

TRILOBITE

AMPHINEURAN
(CHITON)

POLYCHAETE
WORM

COPEPOD

TROCHOPHORE
LARVA

GENERALIZED
PROTOSTOME

ANNELID

ZOANTHARIA

RUGOSE
CORAL

PLATYHELMINTHE
(FLATWORM)

NEMATODE

GENERALIZED
PROTOZOAN

MEDUSOID
(JELLYFISH)

CTENOPHORE
(COMB JELLY)

ALCYONARIA

HYDROID

CONULARID

GENERALIZED POLYP

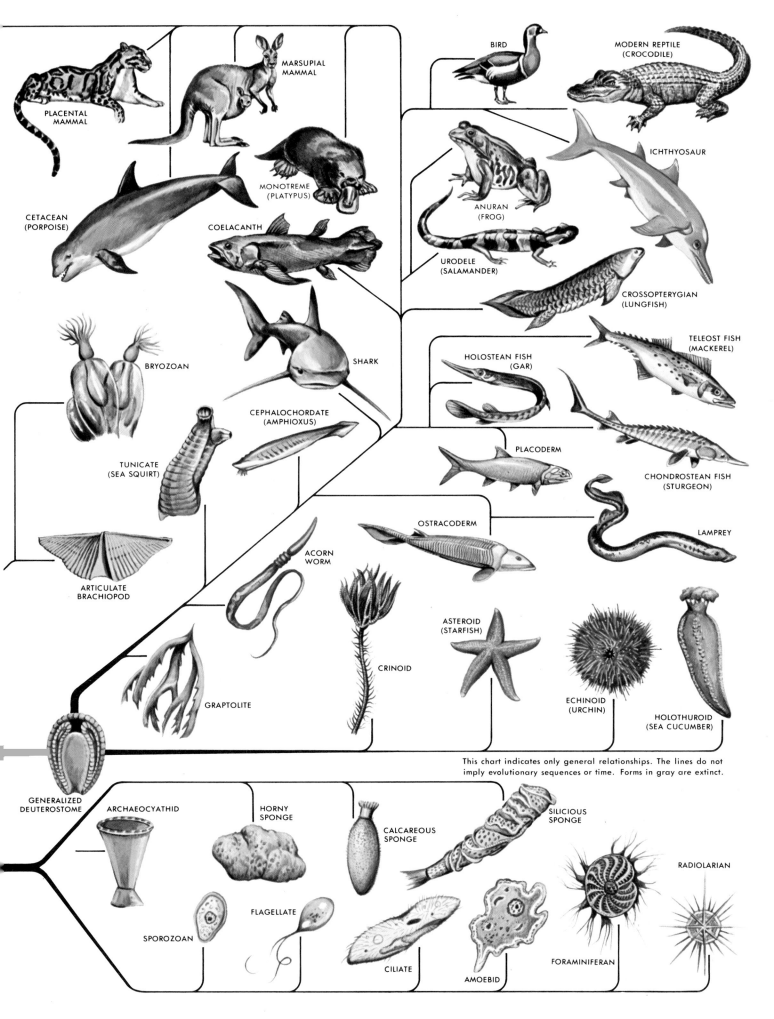

PLACENTAL MAMMAL

MARSUPIAL MAMMAL

BIRD

MODERN REPTILE (CROCODILE)

MONOTREME (PLATYPUS)

CETACEAN (PORPOISE)

COELACANTH

ANURAN (FROG)

ICHTHYOSAUR

URODELE (SALAMANDER)

CROSSOPTERYGIAN (LUNGFISH)

BRYOZOAN

SHARK

HOLOSTEAN FISH (GAR)

TELEOST FISH (MACKEREL)

CEPHALOCHORDATE (AMPHIOXUS)

TUNICATE (SEA SQUIRT)

PLACODERM

CHONDROSTEAN FISH (STURGEON)

ARTICULATE BRACHIOPOD

ACORN WORM

OSTRACODERM

LAMPREY

ASTEROID (STARFISH)

CRINOID

ECHINOID (URCHIN)

HOLOTHUROID (SEA CUCUMBER)

GRAPTOLITE

This chart indicates only general relationships. The lines do not imply evolutionary sequences or time. Forms in gray are extinct.

GENERALIZED DEUTEROSTOME

ARCHAEOCYATHID

HORNY SPONGE

CALCAREOUS SPONGE

SILICIOUS SPONGE

RADIOLARIAN

SPOROZOAN

FLAGELLATE

CILIATE

AMOEBID

FORAMINIFERAN

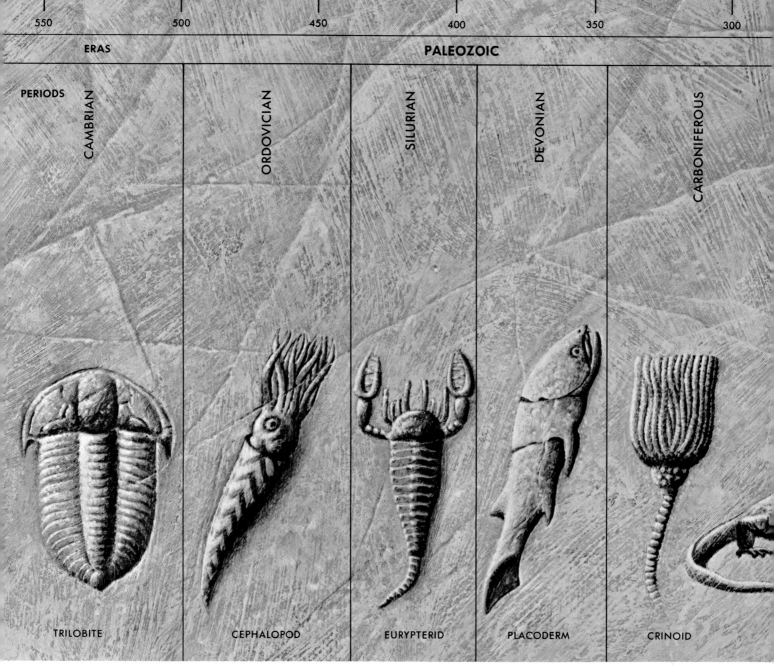

PERIODS   CAMBRIAN   ORDOVICIAN   SILURIAN   DEVONIAN   CARBONIFEROUS

TRILOBITE	CEPHALOPOD	EURYPTERID	PLACODERM	CRINOID

Geologic Time Scale

Written history goes back to about the time of the early Egyptian civilization—roughly 6000 years B.C. Cave paintings can be as old as 50,000 years. The earliest true men lived only a few million years ago. Actually, these time spans are trivial compared to the total age of the earth.

The dinosaurs lived in the Mesozoic era, several hundred million years ago, but they too are relative latecomers. The earliest known life-forms are over three billion years old. To deal coherently with these vast amounts of time, geologists devised the geologic time scale, which breaks up the four- to five-billion year history of the earth into segments usually bounded by some natural lithologic or evolutionary break.

The largest divisions in the scale are *eras*, and there are but four (or five if, as some specialists believe, the recent is adequately different from the rest of the Cenozoic). Within each era are *periods*, the most com-

92

Time for life. The animals shown are characteristic of their period. Before the Cambrian, stretching back to the very beginning, was Precambrian time. It is still mysterious, since there are few good fossils, and is omitted here.

monly discussed units. The Tertiary period of the Cenozoic era is further divided into *epochs*, which are the smallest worldwide subdivisions used in the time scale.

There are a vast number of local or continentwide time and rock-unit subdivisions called formations and stages, but the catalog of these is enormous and food only for the specialist and the serious student.

The names given eras are straight-forward. The suffix *zoic* means "life." Paleo-, meso-, and ceno- mean respectively: ancient,

middle, and recent. Thus the names refer to the general stages of evolution the various living creatures had achieved in each era. Formation names usually describe the location from which came the first described fossils or where the first stratigraphic sections of that age were found.

93

The First Animals

The evolution of life began billions of years ago in the primordial ocean. Over eons the proper combination of proteins, nucleic acids, and enzymes led to a living cell—a creature that was able to take in food, grow, and reproduce its own kind.

Protozoan means "first animal." Flagellata, one group of protozoans, have varied body forms, but all have flagella—whiplike projections that lash about, providing propulsion for the organism. Some, like *Euglena,* contain chlorophyll and are closely related to some microscopic algae.

The amoebas belong to another group of protozoans—the Sarcodinia. It is believed that the amoeba evolved from flagellates which had abandoned their former mode of life. Sarcodinians have evolved into many specialized types. Foraminifera and radiolarians inhabit the oceans. Their skeletons, made up of calcium and silicon compounds respectively, abound on the ocean floor. They have left a good fossil record, dating back to at least the Cambrian period.

The most highly evolved group of protozoans are the Ciliata. Their name is derived from their mode of propulsion— cilia, which are short whiplike structures. Although microscopic, Ciliata show an extremely high degree of internal complexity with a nucleus, gullet for food capture and intake, and vacuoles for storing food and eliminating wastes.

Because Protozoa generally left a poor fossil record, changes that occurred in their past must be inferred from those living today. Most investigators believe the Flagellata were the group from which higher forms of life developed. The progression from one-celled to multicellular organisms was a gradual one. The first step upward was probably the aggregation of single cells in a colony of individual cells, but not yet forming a coherent organism.

Sponges are among the most primitive coherent multicellular organisms. They belong to the phyllum Porifera, or "pore bearers." Sponges show wide variation: large and small, simple and complex. The simplest sponges are vase-shaped, attached to the substrate at their lower end. These sponges have a large central cavity, and millions of microscopic pores connect it to the outside through a large opening at the top of the sponge. Larger, more complicated sponges are elaborations of the same pattern; their

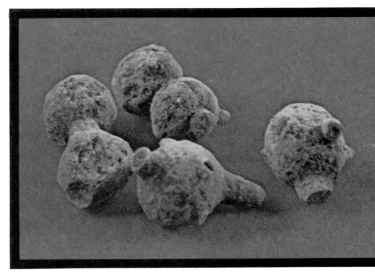

central cavity, however, is usually divided by complex passages. The interior of sponges is lined with flagellated collar cells, very similar to the free-living protozoan forms. The beating of the flagella produce water currents that enter through the tiny pores and exit via the large opening on top. Food and oxygen are extracted from the water and wastes are carried away.

Sponges are a very ancient group. Fossils have been dated back to the Lower Cambrian period. Many scientists believe the presence of collared flagellates indicates that sponges originated from that protozoan stock. It is universally agreed, however, that sponges are a primitive stage in the evolution of multicellular organisms and that they do not form a part of the main evolutionary line from protozoans to higher forms.

Fossil "pop-beads." Sponges usually don't leave good fossils. Girtycoelia (above) is one of the few that can be recognized for what it is.

Form, function, and color. The array of sponge shapes (opposite) shows that form does not limit function of these filter-feeders. Some conform to the substrate; others create bizarre forms of their own, growing straight or curved, thick or thin, to expose themselves to passing currents. The wide variety of sponge colors indicates that color is not important and has no survival advantage for the group.

Multicellular Animals

Any advanced metazoan, or multicellular animal, is very complex in structure, with a variety of body tissues and organ systems. Less complicated forms, like some of those found in the sea, have a simpler physiology. The cells of the simpler metazoans tend to be arranged in three layers: an outer sheet of cells called the ectoderm, a middle layer called the mesoderm, and an inner layer called the endoderm. In still lower metazoans the mesoderm is absent, and the diges-

tive system has only one opening to the outside. Simple animals that abound in the sea today fit this last description—the Coelenterata or Cnidaria.

Coelenterates are often called flowers of the animal kingdom. They are represented by such common forms as jellyfishes, sea anemones, and corals. Two radically different body plans are prevalent in this group. One is a sessile, attached form called a polyp, with the mouth facing upward, and the other is a free-swimming medusa whose body plan is simply an inverted polyp. Corals and anemones have adopted the polyp way of life, while jellyfishes have chosen the medusoid mode of existence. Some members of the group even alternate between the two styles, from generation to generation.

Coelenterate body construction consists of two layers of cells—the ectoderm and the endoderm—held together by secretions of nonliving substances called mesoglia. There is only one opening between the internal cavity and the exterior, and it serves both as a mouth and as an anus.

A characteristic of the phylum Coelenterata is the presence of nematocysts—stinging cells used in defense and food capture. Because higher metazoan forms lack these structures, some investigators are reluctant to term coelenterates as ancestral metazoans. Because they are soft-bodied, coelenterates have left a poor fossil record and ancestral relationships can only be speculated upon. Regardless of their role in evolution, coelenterates, even with their low level of organization, have survived for millions of years.

Reflection in blue. This Pelagia *jellyfish (left) is a simple animal of the same body plan as an anemone but is oriented upside down.*

Flatworms

Platyhelminthes are soft-bodied, usually much flattened worms. Their organization places them somewhere between the coelenterates and annelids, a highly developed group of worms. The smallest flatworms are microscopic, and the largest are the ribbon tapeworms, which spend most of their time in a vertebrate host and may reach a length of 50 feet or more.

Beginning with the platyhelminthes, most higher groups of organisms are two-sided, in other words bilaterally symmetrical. This led to the differentiation of the front end into a sensory center with concentrated nervous tissue and well-developed sense organs, giving bilateral animals an immediate and apparent advantage over lower forms such as coelenterates.

Most flatworms have a digestive cavity. When present, it has only one opening to the outside, as in coelenterates. In place of the jelly that provides much of the coelenterate bulk, flatworms have a solid cellular middle layer—the mesoderm—which includes sets of muscles and a variety of organs. Like the sponges and anemones, flatworms have amazing regeneration capabilities. When cut into a number of pieces, each will develop a head, tail, and full complement of sensory and other organ systems.

It is not clear how the flatworms originated. Because they have soft bodies and few preservable parts, they have left a poor fossil record. Whatever their origin, flatworms are the remnants of a stock of creatures that had a great effect on subsequent evolution.

A flatworm. Without obvious defenses this colorful flatworm seems to advertise its presence (right). A poor fossil record leaves its exact history in doubt.

Worms with Feet

Annelids are the most highly organized worm forms, and members of this phylum include earthworms and seaworms. About 8000 annelid species have been described, the majority of them living in the sea.

Annelids have adopted the bilaterally symmetric body plan. As seen in the more primitive flatworms, this type of symmetry leads to the development of a specialized head region—a center for sensory perception. In *Nereis,* a marine annelid, the formation of a head is not far advanced. However, a set of feelers is present that acts as touch and smell receptors. *Nereis* also has two pairs of eyes. Small yet efficient, they aid the organism in obtaining important information about its environment.

Annelids, in many ways, have expanded and modified the more primitive metazoan body plan as it exists in the coelenterates and plathyhelminthes. Annelids have improved the efficiency of the digestive system above that of flatworms by having two openings to the gut: a mouth and anus. And in *Nereis* a set of pincing jaws which can be thrust out aids the worm in capturing food.

We saw that the coelenterate body was made up of two layers of cells—an outer layer of ectoderm and an inner layer of endoderm. The platyhelminthes added a third layer—the mesoderm—which in the more advanced annelids is arranged in sheets to form a liquid-filled body cavity called the coelom. The coelom appears in all higher forms and allows for more complexity of muscle development and the evolution of more complex organ systems.

The phylum Annelida derives its name from the Latin "anellis," a ring. Visible externally are a series of rings encircling the body, each delineating an internal partition dividing the body into segments. Each segment in *Nereis,* besides containing its own portion of the coelomic cavity, has a pair of kidney like tubules called nephridia that eliminate nitrogenous wastes. Annelids have a closed circulatory system. Each segment receives blood from the paired vessels that run from head to tail. Nerve ganglia, packages of nerve fibers associated with the nerve cord that runs the length of the body, are found in each segment. They deliver stimuli to the head region where a concentration of nerve

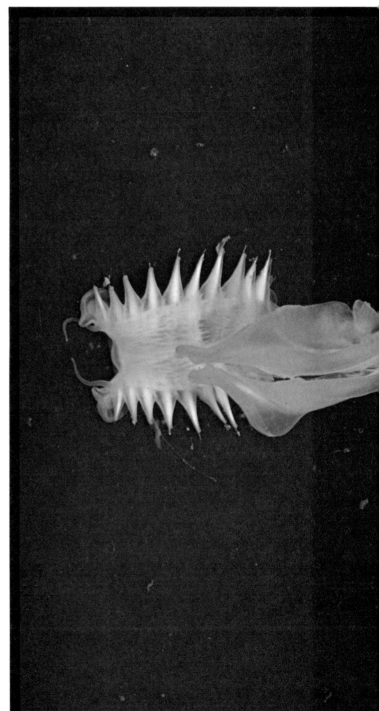

cells have formed a primitive brain that mediates body functions. *Nereis* has developed, or has begun to develop, almost every type of organ found in more advanced forms. Annelids, like most animals with soft bodies, have left a poor fossil record. However, fossilized worm tubes, once the home of sea-dwelling worms, have been uncovered along with a few fossils of the entire creatures and a number of worm jaws. The annelids are an ancient group, originating about 450 million years ago. Because the fossil record is poor, annelid ancestry is debated. Embryological similarities indicate a strong relationship between flatworms, annelids, and a higher group, the molluscs. Annelids take their place in the evolutionary tree of life as the first creatures to have a coelom, a characteristic structure found in virtually all advanced forms of life.

Home is a tube. *The marine parchment worm* Chaetopterus *(below) dwells in a tough-walled tube. This one has been removed to show its appendages.*

On Clams, Snails, and Squid

It is very hard to tell that a mollusc is a mollusc by just looking at it. Molluscs as a phylum include more different-looking creatures than any other group of animals, and any family resemblance between them is often hidden. It is difficult to see that the barely moving blind clam and the graceful squid with its huge eyes and jet-propelled movements are both molluscs. There would seem to be no connection between the soft eight-armed octopus and the hard-shelled snail, yet despite their outward differences, there is no doubt about their family connections. Every type of mollusc has a two- or three-chambered heart, a kidney, gills, and a well-developed nervous system. Not all of them have complete shells, but most have some form or remnant of shells.

Since molluscs are usually, but not exclusively, classified by the appearance or location of the muscular foot or feet they possess, their scientific name is made up of the Greek suffix "pod," which means foot, and various prefixes, which indicate the location of the foot. There are cephalopods, or "head feet" —these include octopuses and squid. Another group is called gastropods, literally "stomach foot"—these are the snails. Pelecypods, or "hatchet foot," are the clam family. There are other names for groups of molluscs as well, based on other attributes of these animals.

The molluscs are an old family whose history can be traced back more than 500 million years to the Cambrian period. They may have existed before then, but there is no fossil evidence to prove it. Small, snaillike shells called *Helcionella* are usually found in Middle Cambrian rocks, and clams too began to leave traces around this time. Finally, in the Late Cambrian period, cephalopods and chitons appeared.

Many of these early cephalopods were often encased in beautiful straight or coil-chambered shells. The first of these known were nautiloids with flat or scooped septa (walls) dividing the individual living chambers of their shells. In later Paleozoic times, the shells developed elaborate dividing walls, perhaps to offer the organism more

The nautilus. *Last of a long lineage that once ruled early seas, the modern nautilus (below) represents one of the rare reversals in evolution.*

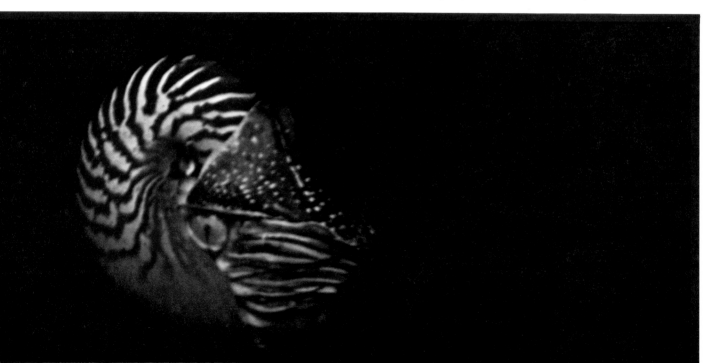

A coil of past life. *Ammonoids (above) replaced early cephalopods in the late Paleozoic and Mesozoic seas, then disappeared without a trace.*

insulation against the stress of deep dives or protection from predators. Such cephalopods with newly evolved shells were named ammonoids. These organisms were dominant through the end of the age of the dinosaurs (the Mesozoic era) during which there seemed to be very few of the original nauti-loids around. For some reason—nobody knows why—all the ammonoids suddenly died out, and only a small group of nautiloids survived, or perhaps became transformed from the complex and seemingly vulnerable ammonoid forms. Sometimes, it seems, the motto of evolution is "Simplify to survive."

Animals with a Past and a Future

If majority rule reigned in the evolutionary world, the arthropods would rule. Over 80 percent of all living species are arthropods, which should give mankind a gentle hint as to the expendability of our species.

Arthropods are the most ancient well-preserved animals that one finds in the fossil record. And trilobites are the oldest known arthropods. Indeed, the classic definition of the Paleozoic period is "that time interval from the first appearance until the final disappearance of the trilobites."

Arthropod means "joint-legged," and this name well describes the most striking feature of this group of animals. But joint-legged can refer to anything from a lobster's claw to a butterfly's antenna to a spider's leg. There are so many varieties of arthropods that the number of insect species alone is in the millions.

In the sea, the trilobites and merostomes were the most widespread forms, but they are now largely extinct (with some exceptions, like the horseshoe crab and the sea scorpion). The crustaceans are the most important living marine arthropods. Crustaceans form most of the zooplankton in the waters of the world and are the second level of the food chain. Plankton of some sort feeds all sea life, at least indirectly, while the larger crustaceans such as crabs, lobsters, shrimp, and crayfish, being higher in the food pyramid, are directly used by man.

Other abundant and prolific forms of the marine arthropods are the barnacles (cirripeda), amphipods, and isopods. Sea spiders, which are not arachnids but pycnogonids, are perhaps the most curious of deep-sea arthropods. Insects never really can be considered sea creatures because none live in the sea, although some occasionally visit it, and the water strider actually walks on the water, using surface tension to hold it up.

In spite of their great numbers, this family of organisms has not left a good fossil record except for the trilobites and the sea scorpions. However, there is enough evidence to suspect that most of the varieties of arthropods have been around from the earliest Paleozoic era—about 570 million years ago. This group's additional claim to evolutionary fame rests on the fact that the true scorpions (arachnids) were the first creatures to venture out of the sea on to the land in the Silurian period. The future of arthropods seems easy to predict. The swarms of insects on land and the hordes of euphausiids and copepods in the sea lead us to the inevitable conclusion that the arthropoda can outbreed and probably outsurvive man.

Living razors. *The beautiful mantis shrimp (left) can slash out with lightning speed, using its razor-sharp forward appendages.*

Creatures of mystery. *Trilobites such as* Bolaspis *(right) appeared, then disappeared leaving no known descendants. They are considered the time-markers of the Paleozoic era.*

Chapter X. Almost a Fish

The routes that evolution takes to accomplish its work are sometimes devious. Important changes in living creatures, with the most far-reaching effects, can often begin in some hidden corner of the sea among common, unspectacular organisms. The development of a cartilaginous structure—called a notochord—is just such a momentous innovation. It is the most important evolutionary step in the history of higher animal life.

"The sea lancelet, with a cartilaginous structure, is a unique stage in evolution."

Fish, birds, whales, and man all have many things in common. But to a marine biologist, the most striking common feature is that each has a backbone. Acorn worms, sea lancelets, tunicates, and a few other not commonly known creatures also have things in common with the vertebrates. These creatures have a notochord present at some stage of their life cycles, and they are chordates. All vertebrates are chordates, but not all chordates are vertebrates. For clear communication we lump the nonvertebrae-bearing forms into a group called protochordates.

This notochord is a curious structure. Let us examine one of the best examples from among the protochordates to see its function. If you are lucky, and observant, you may see a small almost-transparent creature half-buried in nearshore mudflats in the warmer parts of temperate oceans. Or it may be darting around just above the bottom. This unique animal is called the sea lancelet, but it is well known by its generic name *Amphioxus*. On quick glance it resembles a headless sardine. What it represents is a unique stage in evolution. *Amphioxus* is a form with an almost fishlike arrangement of organs and muscles, but it lacks vertebrae and many of the characteristic fin and head structures of fish. It has no stomach. There are many gill bars arranged in a lattice; the sea lancelet feeds by filtering particles from the water. Most important, the notochord alone serves as the structure against which the muscles work. The notochord then is a device to provide leverage.

Other protochordates use the notochords in slightly different ways. The acorn worm uses it as an internal digging stick to help the proboscis burrow into the sea bottom. The tunicate larva uses it in almost the same fashion as the sea lancelet, but for some reason the adult tunicate functions quite well without any trace of a notochord. When the free-swimming tunicate larvae metamorphose into adults, the larval tail which contains the notochord is absorbed and disappears.

A rare and poorly known group of protochordates live in the deep sea. They are colonial and are called pterobranchs. They may be related to a widespread group of extinct forms called graptolites. These colonies of planktonic animals flourished in the Ordovician and Silurian oceans and then slowly disappeared. They most closely resemble the teeth of a sawblade. Some very careful work upon their remains has shown that they contain enough features in common with the pterobranchs to suggest a relationship, and that they may be protochordates. It is odd to think that man is, however distantly, related to floating "sawteeth," headless sardines, or pointy-nosed worms.

The sea lancelet. Amphioxus is an advanced protochordate (above). Internal view (below) shows typical chordate gill slits, a notochord, segmented musculature and a dorsal hollow nerve cord.

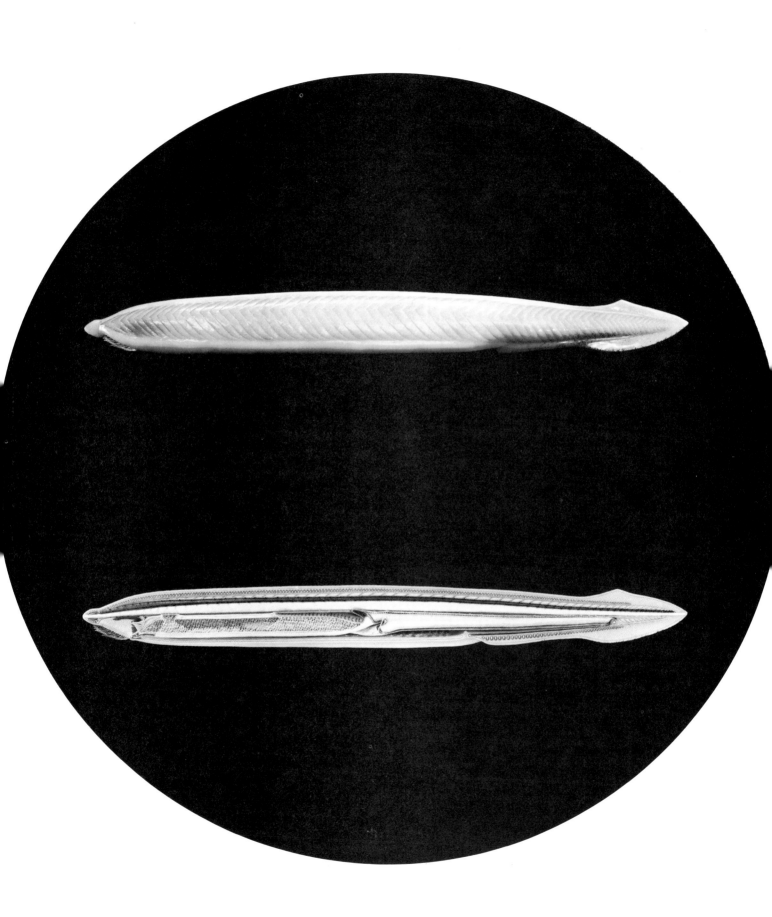

Spiny Skin

Echinoderm means "spiny skin," and the taxonomists who named the group must have been looking at the sea urchins. Any bather or diver who has trod on a sea urchin can attest to the accuracy of the name. Some echinoderms though have soft projections or no spines at all.

There are a variety of forms included in this phylum—the starfish, sea stars, sea cucumbers, sand dollars, crinoids, and forms that exist only as fossils. The echinoderms, espe-cially the stalked forms such as crinoids, have a long evolutionary history, but they have been rather conservative within a distinct pattern. On most members you can see traces of the starfish's fivefold radial symmetry pattern. This simple pattern hides their true evolutionary position.

While being true invertebrates, the echinoderms hover somewhere along the edges of the chordate lineage. There are a number of similarities between the larvae of echinoderms and acorn worms. Starfish and their kin also have a number of advanced features.

Symmetry means the pattern upon which the body is organized. Man is bilaterally symmetrical; that is, each side is the mirror image of the other (excepting the position of the heart and some other organs such as the liver). The starfish has radial symmetry as an adult, based on multiples of five, but as a larva it is bilaterally symmetrical.

Echinoderms have a water-vascular system, which is an analog of the closed chordate internal circulatory system. The other internal structures of the echinoderms show that these animals are not nearly as primitive as they seem. They seem to be an odd mixture of primitive and advanced life.

The starfish has almost legendary regenerative powers. Oddly, this is usually considered a primitive characteristic. But how can one judge? The divers, who thought at first that the crown-of-thorns starfish invasion of the Great Barrier Reef might be stopped if the starfish were simply torn apart, were rather disturbed to discover that they were in fact helping spread the starfish. Most torn parts grew into new ones.

The great masses of late Paleozoic age crinoids are gone. At times they were so numerous that cubic miles of limestone were made up of their skeletons. But the modern crinoids survived. Sea stars and sea cucumbers blanket the deep sea. Our tide pools are full of urchins and starfish. We need not look down upon our distant ancestors—they are well suited to their life-style.

Flower without a stem. Many modern crinoids do not have a stalk, such as this Indo-Pacific species (left). The feathery appendages filter food from the waters passing through them.

Flower of the ancient seas. The stalked crinoid (below) flourished in the early seas. Crinoids were often so numerous that their skeletons formed cubic miles of limestone sediments, which are now rock.

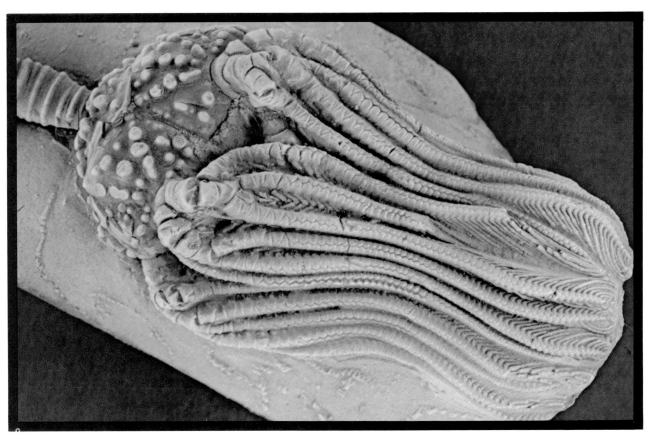

and in the proboscis there is a structure reminiscent of a notochord.

The acorn worm spends its days burrowing through the mud, and it is here that the notochord and proboscis serve it well. The mouth is located on the undersurface of the animal, opening in the collar. The proboscis is stiffened by the notochord and is con-

Making tracks. An abyssal acorn worm (above) was photographed 15,000 feet below the surface. It left a coiled fecal casting on the bottom sediments.

When Is a Worm Not a Worm?

When it's a protochordate, of the subphylum Hemichordata. "Worm" usually refers to both a shape and to a group of animals in several phyla. The acorn worm is a very distant, very aberrant relative of the chordates —some taxonomists would place it in its own phylum. Its "worminess" comes from the shape alone. Elongate, soft, burrowing, and bottom-dwelling, it seems to behave like the usual polychaete worms. But at its front end there are a few strange-looking additions. A collar, looking rather like an acorn's cup, and a proboscis (or "snout") which in some types resembles the acorn itself—hence its name. A dissection reveals some interesting structures, surprising in terms of the outward simplicity of the body.

There is some development of a dorsal (its top in a horizontal view) hollow nerve cord, which is characteristic only of chordates. The throat region has gill slits, which are another definitely chordate characteristic,

Deep-sea camera. We lowered a deep-sea camera system over the edge of Calypso (below), hoping to record the activities of abyssal life. The systems are built with intense stroboscopic light sources.

108

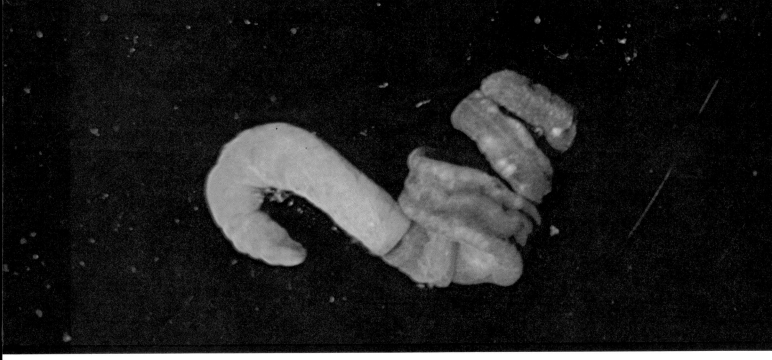

trolled by a muscular system. To make its living, the acorn worm simply digs in with the proboscis, passes the mud it upturns through its digestive passage, and eliminates it. Nutrients are absorbed along the way. Water is passed through the pharynx (throat) via the gill slits, and this is the method of respiration. Generally these worms are small but, as we have seen elsewhere, a few monsters do exist in the deep sea. One abyssal acorn worm found on the bottom in 15,000 feet of water measured over three feet in length. It is reported to feed on ooze collected on strands of mucus secreted by the proboscis; cilia then move them back to the mouth where the food is extracted, leaving the mucus at the collar. Deep-sea photographs revealing obscure tracks or coils of fecal material often mystify scientists. Luckily the cameras periodically spot the animal and thus identify the coil and loop makers. Some of the shallow water species act much like a garden worm does in turning over the soil as they burrow below the surface obtaining nourishment from the rich organic sediments.

The nervous system of the acorn worm is very primitive despite the presence of the dorsal hollow nerve cord. It is not even as

Acorn worm. This creature (above) is an important evolutionary link connecting the invertebrates to animals with backbones.

complex as that of the simple flatworms, although starfish, close relatives of the acornworm, do not have a nervous system of great complexity either. This simplicity may be a secondary development, because after all the acorn worm does not require a complex nervous system to grub through the mud.

The acorn worm larva provides the closest ties between the chordates and echinoderms. It is a top-shaped blob of protoplasm, free-swimming and fitted with bands of locomotive cilia (hairs). It is almost a dead ringer for the larvae of some echinoderms. In fact, some scientists were once very surprised to find their starfish growing up to be acorn worms! This resemblance may be a case of convergence, due to similar life habits, but most biologists would presume there is a relationship between the echinoderms and the hemichordates.

So, unspectacular as the acorn worm may look and unassuming as its life habits may be, our far-removed primate relative can say quite a bit to us.

109

Tunicates

In searching out the ancestors of modern vertebrates, we must descend far down the tree of evolution. An important link in the chordate evolutionary chain are the tunicates, or sea squirts, members of the subphylum Urochordata.

Adult tunicates are quite unlike any vertebrates. They are little creatures, which sometimes float but most of the time are found attached to rocks or other objects in the shallow water. They look like a lumpless mass of protoplasm held together by a tough, leathery skin, or tunic. They are filter-feeders; each has individual incurrent chamber, and in the colonial forms they combine their excurrent chambers in a common sewer. Adult tunicates have no brain or spinal cord; in fact they have very little nervous tissue. They also lack a notocord or any skeletal system. How, then, are tunicates related to vertebrates? Careful examination of the tunicate food-straining apparatus reveals that it is also a complicated gill system through which the organism breathes. This gill system, which is on the level of chordate organization, is the only chordate characteristic exhibited by the adult tunicate. However, vertebrate relationships become apparent upon examining the tunicate larva.

In many tunicates the larval stage resembles a tadpole in shape, with an enlarged head region and slim tail. A dorsal nerve cord and a well-developed notochord are present, and at this point the free-swimming larva is very similar to *Amphioxus*. Eventually, the head region of the larva attaches to the bottom and the larva gives up its active life. The gill region expands and the nerve cord and notochord disappear, resulting in the adult tunicate body arrangement.

These peculiar animals possess some additional characteristics of interest. They are one of the few groups of animals which possess cellulose, an almost exclusively plant-claimed carbohydrate. Cellulose is used as a component of the tunicate's thick tunic. Some members of this group have been found to contain very high concentrations of a rare element—vanadium. Just why or how this chemical is collected is a mystery but the fact remains that tunicates can isolate vanadium much more efficiently than do man's sophisticated systems.

It is not clearly understood which is the more primitive type, the adult tunicate or the larvae. The general consensus among researchers is that ancestral tunicates were sessile, nonmotile, filter-feeding animals that evolved free-swimming larvae whose job it was to "set up shop" for the adult in a new and possibly more favorable environment. It is reasoned that under favorable conditions some tunicate larvae may have remained in the neotenous state, that is, as juveniles, retaining the tail and motile habits throughout life, instead of settling down to the adult stage. This, some researchers believe, set the stage for the evolution of the chordates, which filled the seas with their kind.

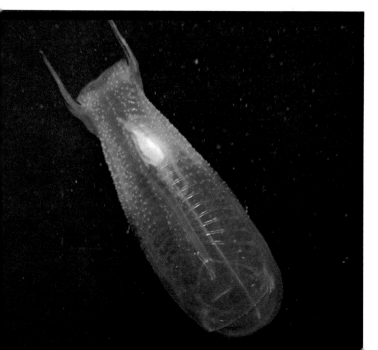

Translucent salp. *This primitive chordate (left) cruises the open sea, forming long chains by budding.*

Communal living. *This colony of ascidians (above) has joined forces to survive.*

A loner. *This tunicate (below) pumps water in one chamber and out the other for filter-feeding.*

Chapter XI. To Have a Backbone

In our everyday speech "spineless" denotes a person lacking in strength and resolution. We are vertebrates and can easily recognize the fact that the spine gives us shape and support and helps keep us upright. What we are not as obviously aware of is that the spine also serves as a point of attachment for the pectoral and pelvic appendages—our arms and legs. The spine is also a point of attachment and leverage for our muscles.

In its blind proliferation of forms, evolution turned out practically all imaginable solutions for life. Larger creatures obtained a rigid support—either an "outer skeleton" (the carapace of insects, lobsters and crabs) or the "inner skeleton" of the vertebrates.

In most adult vertebrates the notochord is replaced by the bony vertebrae. Some primitive vertebrates retain the notochord (lampreys and hagfish, for example), with only

---

"Larger creatures needed a rigid support: an outer carapace or an inner skeleton."

---

a trace of bony tissue growth. Sharks and their relatives never develop true bony tissue; instead their skeletons are composed of cartilage. They represent a separate line of evolution from the primitive jawless fish. But shark, the now-extinct armored, jawless, and jawed primitive fishes, and lampreys are vertebrates rather than protochordates, because they have a definite development of the vertebral column.

Some of the other characteristics of backboned animals are less obvious. All vertebrates, even men, have internal gills and gill slits. Most of the higher vertebrate forms have the gill slits only in the embryonic stage, while the aquatic forms retain them

through life as functional structures. This is in contrast to the lower animals which generally have external gills.

The main nerve cord of the complex invertebrates, such as arthropods and molluscs, runs along the ventral (underside) portion of the animal. Vertebrates have a dorsal (topside on a horizontal-swimming form) nerve cord of all vertebrates is also hollow. protective passage made up by the vertebrae. The position of this cord is very important because it takes many evolutionary steps to move a nerve cord from one side of an animal to the other, and this fact clearly shows that the insects and clams are nowhere near the vertebrate line. The dorsal nerve chord of all vertebrates is also hollow.

In defining a vertebrate, we have noted that they all have their skeletons inside the body, while molluscs, anthropods, and some other invertebrates have external skeletons. Some fish appear to have an external skeleton, but the source of this hard material is nonskeletal tissue. A good example of a hard but nonskeletal exterior is the armor of a trunkfish, which is derived from its scales.

Fish often fossilize extraordinarily well. In the Green River Shales from Wyoming we can find the remains of freshwater fish that lived in a large lake, which was calm enough to allow even and rapid sedimentation, and thus good preservation.

The fish that dies today on the beach stands a passing chance of becoming a fossil if it can avoid the ravages of scavengers and microorganisms that attack dead and dying flesh.

All in the family. Both the fossil fish (below) and grouper (above) have the same basic structure. Both derive internal support from a vertebral column.

The First Fish

If "fish" means a swimming, cold-blooded creature, then the first vertebrates were fish. Technically they are *Agnatha*—jawless animals whose only living direct descendants are the lampreys and hagfish. But in a world where jaws had not evolved, the *Agnatha* were temporary rulers.

In the Ordovician period the trilobites, first masters of the Paleozoic seas, were beginning their decline. Most of the animal groups were represented by the end of the Ordovician, and the remains of a jawless vertebrate of this period have been found in some freshwater sediments in Colorado. The remains

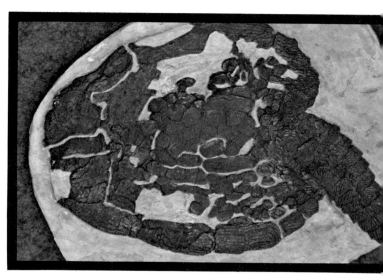

Fossil Agnatha. *Armored ostracoderms, such as the fossil Cordypeltis (above), had skeletons that were mostly cartilage.*

of this primitive fish like creature are very fragmentary, however.

There is another time gap in our knowledge. From middle Silurian age rocks in England come the remains of two genera of jawless vertebrates, *Jamoytius* and *Thelodus*. They were found together in marine sediments, but again the remains are poor.

By late Silurian times the armored ostracoderms (the name means "bony skin") were well established and were filling the oceans. The tails of fish are usually taken for granted by the casual observer as a structure that enables the fish to move. This observation leads to other questions—how fast and in

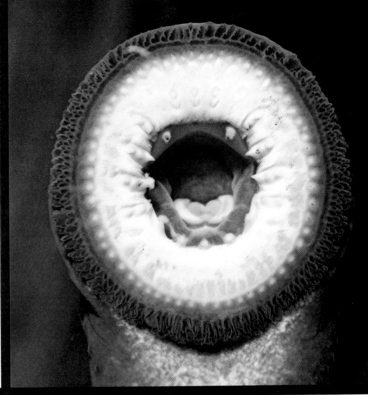

which direction do they move? Without jaws, many ostracoderms had to feed off the bottom, and it would therefore be advantageous to have a tail that would propel the fish downward. Evolution invented just such a tail, called the heterocercal tail. The top part of this forked tail is longer than the bottom. It gives more thrust and down goes the swimmer. Later some forms found it advantageous to dwell in the upper waters and the reverse-heterocercal tail evolved. Most modern fish have a homocercal (even length) tail.

Ostracoderms came in many varieties; some had electric cells, some had projecting spines, and some almost looked like modern fish— but none had jaws. They didn't last long, only through the Devonian period, when they were replaced by the placoderms who had the advantage of jaws. While they lived, ostracoderms bore testimony to the philosophy of making do with what you've got.

Living **Agnatha.** *The lamprey shows a jawless mouth full of teeth (above), which it attaches to hapless living fish (left). It sucks out the body fluids through a hole rasped by its tongue.*

A Giant Step Forward–Jaws

It is inconceivable to talk, eat, drink, or yawn without moving our jaws. Jaws are a most important part of our anatomy, but we do not use our teeth and jaws for defense. Fish and animals do, however, and they also use them to grasp food and other objects, in some cases as we do hands.

The most primitive fish, ostracoderms and their relatives, managed to get by without jaws, but it was a great breakthrough when the first rudiments of jaws appeared.

In primitive fish, there are a series of gill arches, as many as ten in number, formed by several bones. These arches are shaped like forward-opening V's. It doesn't take too much imagination to conceive of strengthening the first V, moving it forward, and chewing with it. Actually it wasn't quite so simple. The first two pairs of arches were eliminated entirely. The third pair of gill arches became

Gaping grouper. Jaws were possibly an important step toward propulsion, since a fish which could bite could pursue and catch a meal (above).

the primitive jaws, while the fourth pair in later fish became a supporting structure for the jaws. The remaining gill arches carried on their original function.

A very nice thing happens when one has jaws—teeth have a strong place to attach. The presence of teeth can allow for totally new and more efficient methods of feeding. All fish from the Devonian onward are jawed, except for the lampreys and sea hags. Today's jawless fishes are parasitic, feeding on the tissues and fluids of living fish. Most jawless ostracoderms were limited to scavenging the sea bottom for food particles.

But with teeth you can attack your prey, and a whole new world of feeding possibilities arose. In the Devonian period, the Age of

116

Fishes, a variety of better-equipped vertebrates evolved, and among them a group of predatory jawed fish arose. They are called arthrodires, and king among them was *Dinichthys* (the name means "terrible fish"). *Dinichthys* was armed with strong jaws and bladelike sheets of bone imbedded in those jaws. They may not have been true teeth, but they worked very well. Specimens are known up to 30 feet long, the head making up about a third of the total length. To bring its teeth into best play, *Dinichthys* had a hinged skull; thus the skull moved up as the jaws moved down. A man could have easily fit in and been cleanly chopped in half. *Dinichthys* did not survive the Devonian period, but it must have terrorized the seas of its day.

Open wide. *The anglerfish (below, left) awaits an unsuspecting prey. A coral trout (below, right) opens up for a cleaner's services.*

Dinichthys and the other arthrodires were part of a group of fish called placoderms, direct descendants of the ostracoderms. Most had armor, and they were generally cartilaginous (as opposed to the bony fish which arose later). The Devonian period was a time of rapid evolution among fish. Forms came and went in relatively short intervals. It was in this period that the lobe-finned crossopterygians dared the land.

Jaws may have appeared in the Devonian period because of the presence of a fierce invertebrate predator—the sea scorpion or eurypterid. These beasts may have forced the ostracoderms into their armor, and the placoderms into their armor and teeth. As the jawed fish arose, the eurypterids declined. It may be a classic case of kicking sand into the bully's face. With the generalization of jawed fish, the Devonian period witnessed a breakthrough in evolution.

To Modern Fish

The placoderms were fishlike, as were the ostracoderms, but they were not true bony fish. The lines of evolution, leading from placoderms to the higher forms of modern fish, are not clear. Somewhere among the primitive jawed fishlike creatures was an ancestor of today's denizens of our oceans. Probably the first thing that comes to the attention of a person who eats a modern fish, such as flounder or cod, is that it has bones.

If sharks and skates were popular foods, we would notice a softer skeleton. Sharks and their relatives are cartilaginous fish (Chondrichthyes), while the remainder of modern fish are bony (Osteichthyes).

The shark group is usually thought of as more primitive than the bony fishes, but actually they both evolved during the Devonian period. The sharks, however, are largely unchanged from the Paleozoic forms. They quickly hit upon some successful formulae for survival: generally live birth; continuous replacement of teeth; swift, aggressive behavior; absence of lungs or swim bladders; and the overall sharklike shape.

The bony fish have a more complicated history. Some of those that stayed in the water cheated a bit (such as the mudskippers and walking catfish) but most remained aquatic, and the group comprising these fish is called the Actinopterygii. The land explorers were the ancestors of the amphibians (and all ter-

Fish in stone. The muds and silts on ocean and lake bottoms can quickly cover up the dead and dying fish, thus preserving them for us (below).

Relic. *The sturgeon (above) is one of the very few remaining chondrostean fish. It would be at home in the seas of 300 million years ago.*

restrial vertebrates) and include coelacanths, lungfish, and a few other exotic forms. Most of this group has been replaced by the more successful of their offspring. The name that applies to most of these fish is Crossopterygii. The lungfish are called Dipnoi.

Unfortunately the names given by ichthyologists (including the name for scientists who work with fish) tend to be jawbreakers. We must beg your indulgence for a few more.

The Actinopterygiians followed a rather neatly straight-line evolutionary scheme. The most primitive forms (Chondrosteans) are characterized by heavy, strong scales and a heterocercal tail (upper lobe longer than the lower). The only living representatives of this ancient group of fish are the sturgeon (a strange living fossil), the birchirs, and a few other rare types.

In the Mesozoic era the holosteans developed from the chondrosteans. They retained heavy rhombic scales but had a newly evolved swim bladder to replace the protolungs of the Chondrostei. All the members of this group are extinct except for the gars and bowfins.

Finally the Cenozoic era presented us with our whole range of modern fish which belong to the group called teleosts. Teleosts range from the smallest minnows to the giant molas and swordfish. They are probably the most numerous and most successful vertebrates that have ever lived, the culmination of 400 million years of evolutionary history.

119

Chapter XII. To Land

For 200 million years life flourished in the sea. With the evolution of jaws and fins, primitive vertebrates became active, aggressive animals. But the greatest evolutionary challenge still lay ahead—the invasion of land. But before truly land-dwelling animals could survive a life away from water a source of food had to be available—plants. Paleontologists tell us that land plants probably developed from unspecialized forms of green algae. But to succeed out of water, plants

---

"What evolutionary changes in the past made it possible for animals to leave the water and survive on land?"

---

needed radical alterations. They required a hard outer covering to resist drying; organs to absorb water and nutrients; spores that could be spread by the wind; and a system of support and conducting vessels that could withstand the forces of gravity. A few sea creatures were able to succeed out of water, and once vertebrates became established on land, they adapted to almost every conceivable habitat and swarmed over the face of the earth. Some took to the air and some even returned to the sea.

What evolutionary changes in the past made it possible for animals to leave the water and survive on land? The remains of early amphibians, the first land-dwellers, have been found in Devonian and Carboniferous rock deposits 350–400 million years old. The evolutionary process is a slow and gradual one, so surely changes were occurring in fishes, making them able to explore land long before the first amphibian appeared.

Lungs were an essential structure for living on land. Gills were very efficient in removing oxygen from water but became useless to animals living on land; without water to support their delicate structures, gills collapsed and dried out when exposed to air. Early in the evolution of bony fishes, the family Dipnoi, or lungfishes, emerged. Modern representatives of this group still retain functional lungs; they are truly air-breathing fish. In fact, some lungfish will drown if they are prevented from breathing air.

In order to live on land and to be able to search for food, animals had to have a way of moving about. Obviously, fins were of little use out of water. The family Crossopterygii, or lobe-finned fishes, were abundant in the Devonian and are believed to be the ancestors of the land vertebrates. Fossil skeletons of these animals are similar to those of early amphibians. Their fins were thick and fleshy, with skeletal elements comparable to the leg of a land animal. It was believed crossopterygians became extinct some 70 million years ago, but in 1938 an Indian Ocean fisherman caught a coelacanth, a member of that family, thought to have been extinct since the age of the dinosaurs.

Modern fishes such as walking catfish, mudskippers, and desert pupfish can live out of water for stretches at a time and are able to move on dry land. Environmental factors that influenced the evolution of these creatures were probably the same ones that caused the first fish to leave the water millions of years ago: pools of water dry up, food becomes scarce, and the fish must find another place to live or it will die.

Out of water. The walking catfish (below) and the mudskipper (above) can travel on land and even obtain oxygen from the air.

Coelacanth

Coelacanths have gained their place in evolutionary history by being considered the forerunner of the first land animals. Their thick, fleshy fins have a simple skeleton but exhibit the basic pattern from which land limbs were derived. At the insertion of the fin is a single bone; two bones are present in the next segment of the fin; and beyond this the bones branch irregularly. This is structurally similar to a human arm, with one bone from shoulder to elbow, two from elbow to wrist, and then a series of bones in the wrist and hand. Bony patterns in the coelacanth skull and braincase also show close relationships to similar structures found in fossils of primitive amphibians.

The first coelacanth was discovered in 1938 by Miss Marjorie Courtenay-Latimer, museum curator of East London, South Africa, who was inspecting a newly landed trawler-load of sharks. In the catch was a strange fish, five feet long, weighing 127 pounds, with a powerful protruding jaw, strong teeth, and padded fins that stuck out like limbs. The trawlermen had hooked it in deep water three miles off the Chalumna River in an area of the Indian Ocean seldom worked by commercial fishermen. The big steel-blue fish had put up a hard fight. Miss Latimer removed the battered find to her museum. Nothing in her ichthyological references resembled this animal, so she sent a sketch of it to Professor J. L. B. Smith of Rhodes University, Grahamstown, South Africa. The fish was badly decomposed by the time Professor Smith arrived to look at it, but he identified it as a coelacanth, a survivor from the age of dinosaurs, thought to have been

Living relict. To the astonishment of scientists a living coelacanth exists. Living in the deep sea, it has yet to be observed.

extinct for 70 million years. He named it *Latimeria chalumnae* to honor the young curator and the place where it was caught. Wanting more coelacanths to study, Professor Smith spread notices that he would reward any fishermen who could provide him with additional specimens. It was 14 years before he saw his second coelacanth, this one caught in 600 feet of water off Anjuan, one of the Comoro Islands. It was a different species from the first and was named *Malania anjouanae*. Comorans had long known coelacanths which they called "gombessa." They prized its flesh as a delicacy and used its tough scales as sandpaper when patching inner tubes of bicycle tires. A few coelacanths have been caught in the decades following that first discovery, all of them around the Comoro Islands—and we have learned more about them. We know

that they are strong, heavy-bodied carnivorous fish that feed on other animals. They reach a maximum weight of about 160 pounds. Though they were fished at night in depths between 650 and 2000 feet, nobody knows where and how they live. Their front and rear fins have been modified into stalked flippers, which probably allow them to walk or creep over the bottom. They have what can be described as a pseudo-lung—lunglike in structure but lined with a thick layer of fat that makes gas transfer difficult. The heart is a very simple structure; the intestine is very similar to a shark's; and the backbone is not bone at all, but rather a cartilaginous rod. Millions of years ago, an ancestor of the present-day coelacanth (such as the one pictured here) moved onto land and gave rise to amphibians and ultimately to all land vertebrates.

Fossil coelacanth. These fossil fish were thought to have become extinct 70 million years ago, until a living specimen was found near Madagascar.

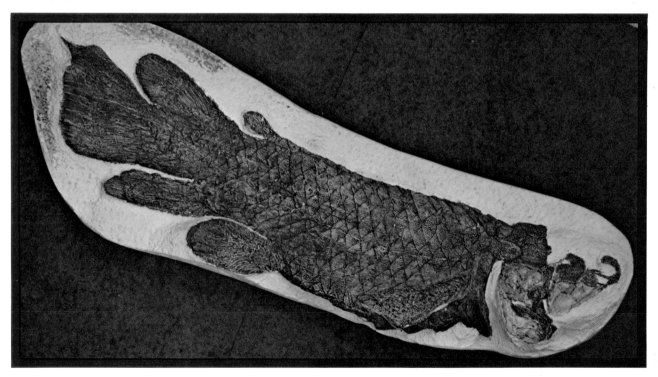

Air-Breathers

Lungfish, members of the family Dipnoi, have been on earth for a very long time. Their fossil remains have been found in Devonian deposits 350 million years old. These fish did not give rise to primitive land vertebrates, and we are therefore again reminded that evolution has no direction and success does not require a total commitment to one specific habitat. At a very early stage in the evolution of bony fish, functional air-breathing organs appeared in the Dipnoi. These organs enabled them to survive in watery habitats where water periodically dried up. Such conditions exist today in great tropical river systems like the Amazon, where during the dry season part of the river system may dwindle to a series of stagnant water holes. Millions of years ago tropical and semitropical conditions prevailed over much of the earth, so this type of habitat was probably widespread. The eventual lack of oxygen in these isolated, shrinking water holes would kill fish unless they were equipped to breathe air.

Fish that lived in such suffocating waters probably began gulping air above the surface—absorbing oxygen through moist skin in the mouth and digestive tract. Evolutionary changes increased blood supplies around the gullet for increased oxygen absorption. Eventually the oxygen-absorbing surface formed a pouch that became long and forked, increasing the amount of surface area for gas transfer. Developing embryos of modern land vertebrates show that, indeed, lungs originate as outpocketings of the digestive tube. Today the distribution of lungfish is limited to three areas of the world:

Unlike the other lungfish, the South American genus, *Lepidosiren,* is absolutely dependent upon air and will drown if held underwater. Before certain Amazon tributaries bake dry, the fish burrows deep into the mud, wraps its tail around its face, and sleeps until the rains come again.

Some researchers argue that the present distribution of lungfish indicates that Africa, Australia, and South America once formed a single landmass. Fossil lungfish have been found in the United States, Europe, and India. Perhaps the surviving groups are the remnants of a once cohesive population that has been separated by continental drift.

A fish that can drown. The lungfish Polypterus (left), in common with the other Dipnoi, must have air to breathe or else it will drown.

A lump of hibernating fish. This African lungfish (below) is encased in a mud cocoon to survive desiccation. This also enables the fish to be airmailed.

Australia, Africa, and South America. The Australian lungfish, *Neoceratodus,* is the most primitive of its kind. Its paired fins are on the end of short stumps, like the coelacanth's, while the fins of the African and South American forms have changed into long, filamentous sense organs. The Australian lungfish is large; it can reach five feet in length and early settlers of Australia used it as food. The lungfish has a good set of lungs, but how it utilizes them is not completely understood.

The African lungfish belongs to the genus *Protopterous.* It flourishes in rivers and swamps from the Nile to the Niger and Congo. In water the fish breathes with its gills, but in the dry season it can burrow into the mud and survive there for as long as three years, even if the mud has been baked to dryness. It does this by breathing air.

Adjust or Walk Out

We have seen how the evolution of lungs and limbs in ancient orders of fish led to their successful invasion of land. The ability of fish to live out of water for long periods of time has also evolved in a number of modern forms. The mudskipper is an interesting little fish that comes on land even though it has no lungs. Mudskippers can be found in the brackish coastal waters of Africa, Australia, and Asia. They spend a great part of their time walking or "skipping" about among mangrove trees at low tide in search of insects, which make up a good part of their diet. Mudskippers flip-flop along on muscular pectoral fins and can travel on land as fast as two miles per hour. They sometimes use their tail for thrust and then leap through the air, covering as much as a yard at a time. In moving about on their pectoral fins, they mimic the pattern of locomotion that the

Two to tango. With periscopic eyes adapted for aerial vision, these mudskippers (below) patiently watch for food or danger.

lobe-finned fishes may have used millions of years ago to get around on land.

Mudskippers have no lungs but can remain out of water for prolonged periods of time because they carry water around with them. The water is stored in spongy sacs near the gills and keeps the gills wet, permitting some "underwater" respiration while on dry land. Because the oxygen is soon exhausted, they are frequently seen dipping their heads into water to recharge the water supply in their spongy sacs. The old idea that mudskippers breathe through their tails has been disproven by scientists. These fish breathe through gills even while they hunt on land —a truly remarkable adaptation.

All the challenges of a changing environment have been met by the small pupfish, no larger than one and one-half inches when fully grown.

When glaciers covered the North American continent from 10,000 to 30,000 years ago, Death Valley was a freshwater lake—Lake Manly. As the glaciers receded, the climate became hotter and drier, and Lake Manly and the tributary system associated with it began to go dry. Of the various species of fish inhabiting the lake only one had the capacity to endure the changing environ-

Fish out of water. This mudskipper (above) is far from being helpless out of water. Spongy sacs keep its gills moist, enabling it to breathe in air.

ment. They were the fittest and have been able to survive to this day in isolated areas where the supply of water has never failed. Pupfish can tolerate a wide range of temperature and salinity fluctuations. Desert streams and pools can be covered with ice on a winter night and rise to over 100° F. on a hot summer day. The salinity tolerance of these animals is also impressive. They can flourish in the fresh water of thermal springs as readily as in desert marshes where the salinity is near that of seawater.

Pupfish have a high rate of reproduction and can successfully maintain small breeding populations. One such population lives in a long narrow spring only two inches deep at the deepest point. The entire pool contains about 80 gallons of water, barely enough to fill the average bathtub. The inhabitants of this spring have been cut off from the nearest pupfish population for perhaps thousands of years. Only the high reproductive capacity of the pupfish enables it to survive in this environment. The only environmental condition that this amazing little fish has not adapted to—the absence of water.

Amphibians

The first true land-dwelling creatures were the amphibians. Approximately 350 million years ago, some crossopterygians began to venture out on land. Mutations had prepared these fish for the transition by providing them with lungs, so they could breathe air, and heavy, fleshy fins, so they could flop about on hard ground.

In Greenland paleontologists unearthed the remains of an animal more advanced than any crossopterygian. Named *Ichthyostega,* it is one of the most primitive amphibians, combining a fish tail with sturdy legs and feet instead of fleshy fins. With "walking legs" *Ichthyostega* could move over the banks of streams and rivers and feed on a newly developed source of food—insects.

The first amphibians were essentially lobe-finned fishes with limbs that had evolved into legs useful for mobility on land. Since there were no other vertebrates on land to compete with, amphibians flourished. For 100 million years they evolved into numerous species and became widespread. Their fossil remains have been found in North America, Europe, Asia, and even Antarctica. Amphibians, throughout the course of evolution, have never wholly freed themselves from the water. Even today, most return to the water to breed. Their eggs are small and have only a jelly coat to protect them. Larval stages, intermediates between eggs and adults, are strictly dependent upon water for survival. Frog larvae, or tadpoles, have a well-developed tail for swimming and breathe by gills. As the larvae reach maturity metamorphosis occurs: gills disappear, lungs and legs develop rapidly, and the tadpole becomes a frog—an air-breather and land dweller. It is interesting to observe that some modern amphibians appear to be evolving away from this double mode of life. In many instances, the tadpole stage has been eliminated and the young hatch from the egg as full-fledged, but miniature, frogs or salamanders.

From the position of fossil remains, it is evident that the early amphibians were very much aquatic animals and still lived side by side with the crossopterygians. We have a Lamarckian tendency to ask such questions as: Why did primitive amphibians develop limbs and become land dwellers? Was it out of a necessity to breathe air, or to find a new source of food, or to escape from enemies? Many investigators are coming to a paradoxical conclusion—limbs that developed by chance enabled amphibians to remain in the water! The Devonian period, in which amphibians originated, was a time of

seasonal droughts. Yet, even when isolated pools became stagnant, the amphibians had no advantage because the lobe-finned fishes could breathe air too by coming to the surface. When food supplies became depleted, a desperate situation arose which would be further complicated if the pool should go dry. If and when this point was reached, the amphibians were at an advantage; with their newly developed land limbs they could quickly travel overland and reach another pool where they could again take up an aquatic existence. Land limbs were seemingly developed because they permitted the animal to stay in water, not to leave it.

Their mode of reproduction has linked amphibians to water and to the past. Because of their dependence upon water, they are likely to remain a simple and relatively unimportant group of animals.

Legged fish. The development of these tadpoles alludes to their history. They begin life fishlike and hatching from an unprotected egg in an aquatic environment. They have elongated tails and successfully derive their oxygen from the water medium. As development proceeds, legs begin to form, the tail is absorbed, and they develop the capability to breathe air. Like their ancestors, they can travel from one pond to another in search of food or to avoid a dwindling water supply.

Chapter XIII. Know Thine Ancestors

Perhaps the one question that has most intrigued man since he began to think is: Where did I come from? The science of evolution arose to answer this question. Before evolutionists there were shamans, theologians, wisemen, philosophers, and many others who proposed various theories to describe the source of humanity. But it was not until evolutionary science began that the mechanisms and specific processes of the gene and chromosome were understood.

Today there are a wide range of scientists who study evolution—among them, biologists, paleontologists, anthropologists, chemists, physicists, and geneticists. They seek to answer the larger and smaller questions—not only "whence comes man," but also such questions as "whence comes the parabolic shape of the ommatidium of *Limulus*." Science seeks knowledge, and scientific research combines an experimental approach (testing hypotheses by experiments) with empiricism (employing observations made in natural circumstances).

Evolutionary science begins with the organic chemists, because they seek answers to the chemical basis of life and deal with the initial "stages of the life from matter" concepts. The chemists and molecular biologists together study the workings of the cell and its nucleic acids—DNA and RNA. Maybe tomorrow a much more refined understanding will be attained, showing that such substances are not the only factors for heredity. Comparable advances in nuclear physics have shown that the building blocks of the universe were far more numerous than the well-known proton, neutron, and electron. Molecular biologists seek further information about the essential substances of evolution by studying the cell.

Geneticists work with the genes and chromosomes—combinations of nucleic acids in the cells of living tissues. They deal with evolution and heredity in living organisms as well as in the test tube.

Physicists collaborate with many of the evolutionary scientists to add depth to the information on the dynamics of evolution and life. Again energy is revived as the starting

---

"The quest for the origins of man is carried out in space and time."

---

and continuing source of life's spark. The metabolism of food, for example, provides the release of certain amounts of energy. The measure of this energy and the comparison of better methods to use nutrients are important parts of determining the evolution of early life.

Paleontologists and other geologists are concerned with the record of past life as preserved in rock. They have the important time perspective firmly in mind, and they have the materials to actually see the evidences of evolution before them—such as the change with time of a fish to an amphibian. The paleontologist is a person who must always think in four dimensions.

Finally the anthropologist directly explores the physical history of man as well as the changes in his culture. There are not an extraordinary large number of human fossils because men generally do not die in places where fossilization is likely to occur.

Man and God. Michelangelo's vision of man's creation is more than slightly at odds with the modern concept of the evolution of Homo sapiens.

131

Wizardy in Modern Laboratories

The mad scientist stares down his microscope barrel. Behind him caldrons seeth, sparks crackle, a raven perches on a dusty skull in the corner. The scientist cackles, "At last I have created life."

This picture, is farfetched, but the creation of primitive life in a laboratory is possible. Dr. S. L. Miller, while working on his doctoral research, devised a method to find out just what may have happened on the primitive earth. He wanted to know if the organic chemicals of living tissues could be synthesized from a mixture of gases which might have been in the earth's primitive atmosphere some four billion years ago.

The gases were those that come out of volcanoes, the suppliers of our early atmosphere. This mixture consisted of carbon oxides, hydrogen, methane, and ammonia. Dr. Miller placed this recreated atmosphere in a closed chamber, had it percolate through water, and subjected it to 60,000-volt sparks from a Tesla coil. The Tesla coil is a simple device for producing high-voltage sparks. The setup was refluxed (recycled through a series of operations) for various periods of time, up to a week.

The sparks from the coil simulate the unshielded earth's lightning discharges, and the refluxing condenses time. Miller had created a model of the primeval ocean and atmosphere and let it work. And it did work.

A working model. The apparatus shown here can be set up in any laboratory, and it can re-create the experiment performed by Dr. Miller. The primary equipment consists of a Tesla coil to produce high voltage sparks; a large flask fitted with electrodes and filled with water and a mixture of gases that simulate the primitive earth's atmosphere; and a source of heat to start the whole process going. You too can create life.

After about a week of operation, the water had turned dark and cloudy, and it contained a mixture of amino acids and other organic compounds. Miller had demonstrated the creation of the basic substances of life from volcanic gases and water.

Since then other scientists have synthesized proteins, enzymes, and more complicated life-substances from inorganic matter. Very recently geologists have been turning their attention to the discovery of fossil amino acids in very ancient rocks, meteorites, and perhaps soon in lunar samples. Very old rocks are known to have spores and particles of algae—some more than three billion years old—but the work on fossil organic compounds can uncover traces of life even if no fossils are known.

Meteorites landing on earth often contain carbon compounds, suggesting that the early stages of life may be organizing somewhere out in space. Or perhaps they are all that's left of a preexisting life-form, known to us only by meteorites which were trapped by the earth's gravitational field.

In dealing with these ghostly traces of life, the chemist must be careful to avoid contaminating the objects he examines. A fingerprint contains amino acids, proteins, fats, lipids, sugars, and salts. We exhale life chemicals with each breath. Dust contains living spores and pollen. A shred of rubber glove contains long-chain carbon compounds. All may lead to misinterpretations, if they get in the wrong places.

The modern wizard who delves into life's secrets must work in a spotlessly clean and dust-controlled laboratory. There is no room for ravens, ancient almanacs, or bottles of frog's tongues in man's latest quest to create life in the laboratory.

The Earliest Evolution of Man

If the geologic time scale were drawn 1000 feet long, the portion occupied by the animals that have left readable records (the period from the Cambrian to the present) would take up about 127 feet. The part occupied by man (the Pleistocene period) would be about five inches long.

One misconception—that man evolved from the apes—has plagued anthropologists for years. But modern anthropoid apes are not man's ancestors; rather man and apes evolved from a common ancestor, who was undoubtedly quite apelike. And there was undoubtedly no one single common ancestor, but rather a whole series of intermediary ape-man steps. We evolved from the same gene pool as did the apes. The modern gorillas and chimpanzees are very much specialized and are part of the line of man's descent. Manlike fossil apes are known from the middle Cenozoic period. The fabled "missing link" may be among these apes, but we will never be sure. Most likely a number of trials and errors occurred, and the lineage that

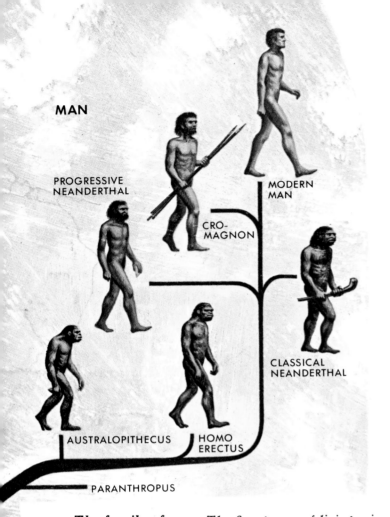

MAN

PROGRESSIVE
NEANDERTHAL

MODERN
MAN

CRO-
MAGNON

CLASSICAL
NEANDERTHAL

AUSTRALOPITHECUS

HOMO
ERECTUS

PARANTHROPUS

The family of man. The five groups of living primates range from the primitive Prosimii, some of which resemble rodents, to the great apes and man himself. The New World monkeys have prehensile tails and are generally more primitive than the Old World monkeys. The direction of evolution that this tree seems to imply must not be misinterpreted to mean that man is primate perfection.

produced the first early man derived its roots from several family trees.

A fossil ape named *Proconsul* seems to be the closest thing to a missing link. It may have been bipedal (erect and walking on two legs), and it shows some brain development beyond the "pure ape" stage.

The question is clear—what makes an ape-like creature a prehuman? Most anthropologists would rank bipedalism as the first criterion. One effect of this form of locomotion is that the hands are free to develop as tool manipulators instead of walking or tree-swinging aids. And we have seen in Volume VIII, *Instinct and Intelligence,* that hands are one of the four essential requirements for candidates to civilization.

But *Proconsul* was still very apelike. Before the Pleistocene period there were a number of apes with prehuman features. In Italy a form called *Oreopithecus* was found; it had a well-developed brain and probably almost erect stance. From a Chinese apothecary shop came the teeth of an enormous creature called *Gigantopithecus*. These teeth were being sold as "dragon's teeth" to be used in medicine and aphrodisiacs when an anthropologist named Von Koenigswald found them. We are not sure if *Gigantopithecus* is close to the central line of man's evolution, but it is the largest ape (12 feet tall) known.

Europe produced many prehuman apes besides *Oreopithecus*. A well-known form called *Dryopithecus* had the earliest characteristic cusp pattern in its molar teeth that help us identify other teeth in our lineage. From Fayum Egypt came many early primates; *Propliopithecus* is considered a "missing link" candidate. *Pliopithecus*, from Europe, though similar in name, is an early gibbon.

There are now so many known prehumans that the best explanation of our "gene pool" suggests a polyphyletic (literally "many lines") origin. We may share the lineage of several of these fossil apes.

Definite early humans did not make their appearance until the Pleistocene period. But our early ape ancestors had spread around the Old World, and certainly must have been important creatures of their day. Considering how destructive modern man is, perhaps our less-skilled forebears could be considered the more civilized, since we find so little evidence of his activity.

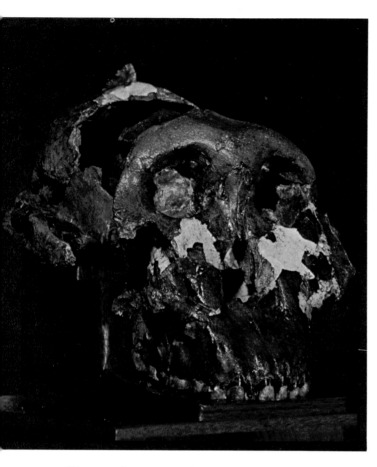

Nutcracker man. *One of the earliest humans is* Zinjanthropus, *often called "nutcracker man." Most anthropologists consider him an offshoot of the line that led to modern man.*

Man Emerges

In 1924 a small skull was found in South Africa. It was that of a human infant, but it was far more primitive than any seen before. Then more remains turned up of mature individuals, some of them gorilla size, some chimpanzee size. All were human but were amazingly primitive. Similar forms were found in East Africa in the Olduvai Gorge.

The remains of the smaller forms were those of the earliest known men, and they are now called *Australopithecus* (although they went through a series of names as each discovery was considered to be a new form of fossil man). The larger gorilla-size creatures seem

to be an evolutionary dead end. They are placed in the genus *Paranthropus* and are not considered direct ancestors of modern man. All of these walked erect and made tools. They hunted in cooperative bands, probably used fire, and may have had speech.

The australopithecines had much smaller brains than modern man. Even when proportions to body weight were considered, the relative volume of the brain wasn't more than half that of modern man. There are additional primitive characteristics such as the lack of a chin, the presence of large canine teeth, a heavy ridge of bone on the skull beneath the eyebrows, and a generally "ape-like" appearance. One of the falacies that has been spread about early man is that they walked stooped over. That bridge was probably crossed, in an evolutionary sense, about the time of *Proconsul*. Had this important step not preceded the humanlike development, *Homo* as we know him could not have preceded this far. Once erect walking was achieved, it must have been fully completed early in the development.

The well-known remains of the Java man and Peking man were the first evidence about the next stage in human development. Fossils of this level of evolution are classified in the same genus as man—*Homo*—but in the species *erectus*. At this point we had grown to approximately the same size as we are today; brains had become bigger (about two-thirds the size of modern man); and the tool-making abilities had reached a far more advanced level than the simple chipped pebble tools created by *Australopithecus*.

Remains of *Homo erectus* have been found in East Africa in beds of rock younger than those which revealed his forebearers. At Olduvai Gorge the succession of progressively more advanced forms is demonstrated up to the upper levels of the *Homo erectus* stage,

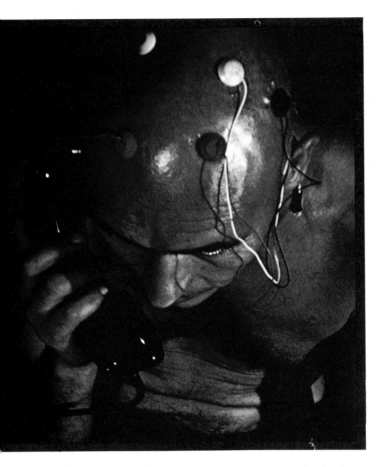

***Future man?** Instead of altering our physical nature will future advances in human evolution dwell on refining our mental capabilities? Or will man direct evolution himself?*

then the record stops. But this does not mean that we have no evidence of what happened next. We do, but from many scattered places, and nowhere is there a continuous set of fossils tracing man from the beginning.

The Neander River flows through western Germany, and it was in the last century here that workmen blasting the limestone cliffs uncovered a heap of bones that turned out to be those of early men. A skull of this evolutionary stage had been found in Gibralter, but as often happens, had been ignored. These Neanderthals (as they were called) were a widespread race of men, now known from Africa, Europe, and Asia. They may have coexisted with modern man, and they may have been our direct ancestors. The characteristics that distinguish Neanderthal man from modern man are impressive, but if a Neanderthaler were dressed in a suit and tie, he probably could pass for a rather rugged-looking businessman. The difference between modern man and the Neanderthal are mostly in proportion and prominence of features: the chin of Neanderthal man receeds strongly, the skull is lower and longer, the forehead slopes back, the brow ridges are heavy. The bones of the Neanderthal body are more bowed, indicating not that he had poor posture, but rather that he had evolved room to fit in strong muscles. His brain capacity was equal to or exceeded that of modern man. Of course, we have no idea about the amount of hair or the exact details of facial expressions in forms known from fossils, but most reconstructions tend to overemphasize the primitive aspects. We would suspect that *Homo erectus* and *Homo sapiens neandertalensis* were no more covered with hair than we are.

There were two general groups of Neanderthals: those who had the more extreme development of their racial features (because the differences that exist between modern and Neanderthal man are not more than racial differences) and those who were more generalized. We came from various mixtures of the generalized group. Early modern man may have interbred with the "classic" Neanderthals too.

When modern man (*Homo sapiens sapiens*) spread throughout the world, he may have killed off the Neanderthal populations, interbred with them, or ignored them. But ultimately he replaced or absorbed them, and since that time, our evolution has been entirely cultural. The famous Cro-Magnon fossils were modern men, differing from us only in small details. Thus by about 30,000 years ago we were there.

Chapter XIV. Sorcerer's Apprentice

The test-tube baby is an adventure in tomorrow's evolution. It has been painted by science-fiction writers as the ultimate horror; but remember, it isn't necessary to create uniform robot-people in the laboratory. Actually some of the mass media and conditioning techniques can approach this today. What the *ex vivo* (out of life) baby could have is a guaranteed genetic pedigree, advanced immunity to diseases, little chance of birth and other inborn defects, and a greater potential for happiness by having aptitudes in which he can find fulfillment.

"Moral and social problems are the major obstacles to genetic manipulations."

It is not as much the technique of genetic manipulation as the moral and social aspects that will be the major obstacle. But it is certain that the future needs of society will be so pressing that we will find solutions.

But as man has turned his gene-altering knowledge to other forms of life, he has shown no such squeamishness and been exceedingly successful. We have strains of corn, rice, and wheat preadapted to succeed in unnatural climatic conditions. They can actually produce more than the wild stock in an optimum environment. Animal husbandry has given us cows that produce abnormally high quantities of milk and chickens that lay more and better eggs. The variety of horse and dog breeds attests to man's ability through selective breeding to bring out or suppress certain qualities. A pitfall of this excessive inbreeding is the loss of natural variation in a strain and a resultant vulnerability to disease. An important aspect of future genetic manipulation will

be to restore by laboratory means the variability promoting various other traits.

Mariculture is beginning to employ the products of genetic research to yield higher outputs of protein, and some of the newly created fish are as odd as the natural experiments in evolution.

There are two important elements to the creation of advanced living forms. First, the genetic aspect must be handled before the creature is born—obviously a gene structure can be altered most easily when it is a single cell about to divide into a whole body.

Then, the upbringing is of primary importance. For years biologists and sociologists argued about which aspect of human child-raising was the most important—eugenics (ancestry) or euthenics (living conditions). Do the children of creative people become creative because they were endowed with good genes or because they had stimulating homelives as children? It now seems that both are almost equally important.

And so in mariculture and farming, the improved seed stock must be treated with improved methods of nurture to allow the potential locked up in the chromosomes to emerge. But genetics can go beyond food. Our ideas of developing a human who is perfectly adapted to an aquatic life may actually be realized at some future time when our biologists begin to experiment with human chromosomes. The dangers of abuse are present, but the day will probably come when our needs will leave no alternative.

"Garden of Earthly Delights." In the sixteenth century Hieronymus Bosch depicted strange distortions of the human figure in his masterpiece.

Man–Unnatural Selection

Today man is able to control and direct the evolution of many animals. In general, man's aim has been to increase the products or capabilities of a certain animal or plant species. Comparison of any domestic animal to its nearest relative in the wild dramatically reveals that man rather than nature decides the qualities of fitness in domestic species. In other words, he decides which individuals have desirable characteristics and therefore should be allowed to reproduce and perpetuate those attributes in their offspring. There are a number of traits man can choose to foster in domestic species; among them are rapid reproduction, plumpness and meatiness, fast growth, and resistance to disease. Such qualities are desirable because they allow a greater amount of total protein production in a given amount of time and space.

The Japanese lead the world in mariculture. This should not be surprising since they derive a greater proportion of their food from the sea than any other major nation. The first species they cultivated on a commercial scale was the yellowtail. Although yellowtails are fast-swimming, open-ocean fish, the Japanese have successfully reared them from larvae to adults in submerged cages. But still no commercially important saltwater fish has ever reproduced in farms or in tanks. The yield of yellowtails has ranged up to 126 tons per acre per year or 62 pounds of fish per square yard. Japanese also cultivate puffers, porgies, filefish, and eels. Many scientists regard the success of the yellowtail farms as proof that sea farms in coastal waters can produce millions of fish annually.

The Japanese are also well known for the strange and exotic fish they have produced as a result of selective breeding. About 1000 years ago the Chinese and Japanese were domesticating the wild goldfish, a rather drab brown, carplike fish. Since then, they have carried on a process of selective breeding that has produced most of the goldfish varieties we know today. Some have trilobed tails and are brightly colored; others look more strange and grotesque. The blackmoor has bulbous eyes that protrude from its head, while the lionhead has tumorous growths covering its front. Some of these highly aberrant varieties are very difficult to raise, and a grower can demand and get several hundred dollars for a perfect specimen. Japanese carp are also famous. While most mature carp are about 12 inches, the Japanese have produced a variety that has reached a length of 40 inches and a weight of 60 pounds.

In these instances, man has taken a hand in evolution to produce many and varied kinds of creatures. This ability to control evolution—to direct its flow and point it in specific directions—has drastically increased our responsibility toward future generations.

Beautiful monsters. *These unnatural-looking goldfish would fare poorly in the wild. Man has directed their evolution, and his criteria determine survival of the fittest.*

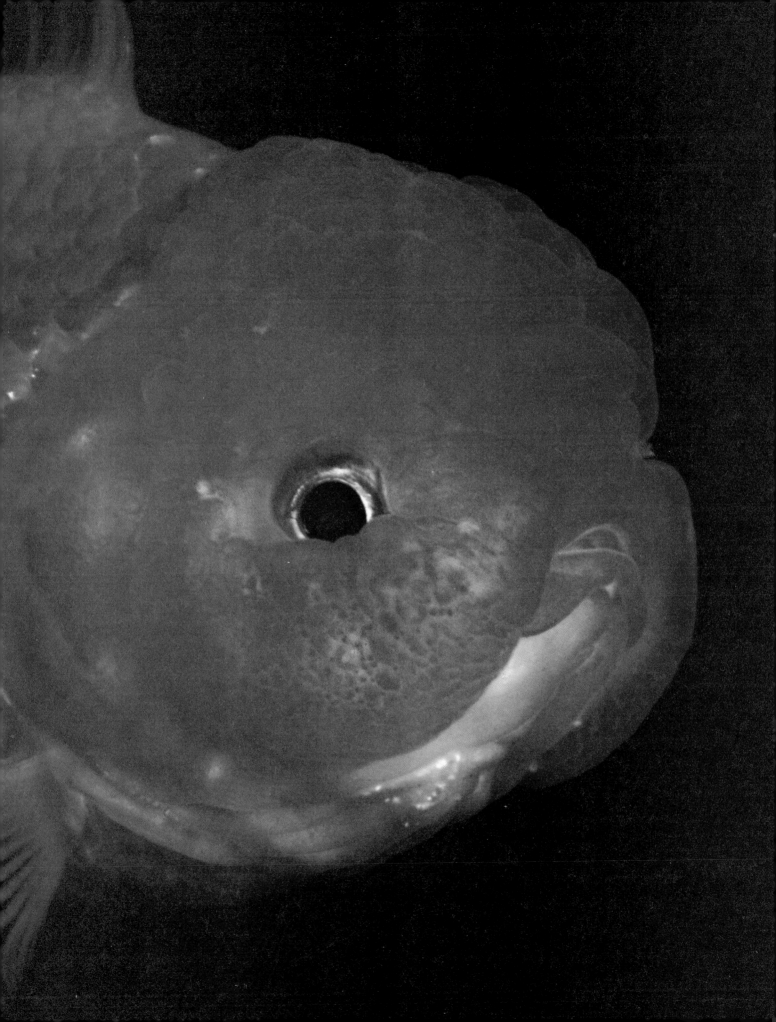

Fickle Winds

Oh! Human day—fly!
What obsessing anxiety frets your heart out?
Are you not gratified to trace your ancestry
Back to your forefathers? Relentlessly you seek
Your very origins ... is there a single drive,
A steady wind that blew from primeval cells to you?
Is life an alphabet, numbered through the ages,
Laboriously ending just with a human Z?
Or may evolution be toying with beings
Like fickle winds with leaves?
Our thirst would not be quenched
If we uncovered all the secrets of our earth!
Already we probe deep into our galaxy
For whiffs of life to be.
Beginnings are beyond—the mystery elsewhere,
Both deeply entombed in the essence of matter.
From the most elusive, tiny grain of substance
Another life may spring to untold destinies,
Away from human quest,
Blown by the Fickle Winds.

Index

ILLUSTRATIONS AND CHARTS:

Howard Koslow—17, 24-25, 39, 92-93, 134-135; Howard Koslow and Paul Singer—90-91.

PHOTO CREDITS:

American Museum of Natural History—105; John Boland—40, 41, 94 (top, left); Bruce Coleman Inc.: Jen & Des Bartlett—2-3, 125 (bottom), Jane Burton—27, 101, 102, 120 (top), 126, 128, 140, R. I. M. Campbell—136, Bruce Coleman, Inc.—14-15, 127, John S. Flannery—118, Jerry Lesser—81, Oxford Scientific films—43, 80 (bottom), 85, 114-115 (bottom), Alan Root—20; Ben Cropp—117 (right); European Art Color Slide, Peter Adelberg, Inc.—139; Freelance Photographers Guild: Dennis L. Crow—78-79, Tom Myers—18, 141, Hugh Spencer—129 (bottom); Bruce C. Heezen and Charles D. Hollister, *The Face of the Deep*, Oxford University Press, 1971—108 (top); Richard C. Murphy—11, 26, 32-33, 38, 44-45, 46; NASA—72; Naval Photographic Center—13; Pellegrini, M. Grimoldi, Rome—131; Vincent F. Penfold, Montreal Aquarium—19; Photography Unlimited: Rick Gregg—67; Carl Roessler—117 (left); Dr. David Schwimmer—12, 62, 65 (bottom) 89, 95, 103, 107, 114 (top), 123, 132; The Sea Library: Ed Angell—69, Francois R. Brenot—113 (bottom), Ben Cropp—48, 82-83, Jack Drafahl—28-29, Henry Genthe—34, Daniel W. Gotshall—110, Hyperion Sewage Plant—80 (top), 86, Tom McHugh—124-125 (top), Tom McHugh, Shedd Aquarium—119, Tom McHugh, Steinhart Aquarium—53, 115 (top), 116; Chuck Nicklin—97, Elliott Norse—37, G. A. Robilliand—59, Carl Roessler—54, 55, 56, 57, 64-65 (top), 68, 94, (bottom), 94 (top, right), 106, Dr. C. W. Sullivan—70, 75, 87, Ron Taylor—111 (bottom), Valerie Taylor—111 (top), Ed Zimbelman—47; Deboyd L. Smith, West Coast Plankton Studies—50-51; Tom Stack & Associates: G. Mathew Brady—5, Joel Cole—49, Dr. E. R. Degginger—21, 84, Keith Gillett—98-99, Bill Noel Kleeman—71, 76-77, Dr. Lloyd McCarthy—23, Tom Myers—96, 120 (bottom), 129 (top), Kenneth Read—36, 142, Shabica—58, Joey Thompson—22, Western Marine Laboratories—61; Taurus Photos—63; Wards Natural Science Establishment, Inc.—109.